Test Practice – Prima

Table of C

		Student Pages
About the Program		
Scope and Sequence Charts	T4	
Introducing Students to Test Practice	T6	
Directions for Units		

Unit 1 Word Recognition
    Lesson 1: Recognizing Beginning Sounds   T7   1
    Lesson 2: Recognizing Ending Sounds   T8   2
    Lesson 3: Recognizing Vowel Sounds   T8   3
Unit 1 Test   T9   4

Unit 2 Reading Vocabulary
    Lesson 4: Matching Words with Similar Meanings   T11   7
    Lesson 5: Matching Words with Opposite Meanings   T11   8
Unit 2 Test   T12   9

Unit 3 Reading Comprehension
    Lesson 6: Understanding Sentences   T12   11
    Lesson 7: Reading Stories   T13   12
Unit 3 Test   T13   18

Unit 4 Math Concepts
    Lesson 8: Working with Numeration   T14   25
    Lesson 9: Understanding Patterns and Relationships   T15   26
    Lesson 10: Working with Measurement   T16   27
    Lesson 11: Working with Geometry   T17   29
Unit 4 Test   T18   31

Unit 5 Math Problems
    Lesson 12: Working with Number Sentences   T20   36
    Lesson 13: Solving Problems   T21   37
    Lesson 14: Working with Statistics and Probability   T22   39
Unit 5 Test   T23   41

Unit 6 Math Procedures
    Lesson 15: Using Computation in Word Problems   T24   44
    Lesson 16: Using Computation   T25   45
Unit 6 Test   T26   46

Unit 7 Language
    Lesson 17: Building Listening Skills   T27   48
    Lesson 18: Prewriting, Composing, and Editing   T28   49
    Lesson 19: Finding Misspelled Words   T32   55
Unit 7 Test   T33   56

Comprehensive Tests
    Test 1: Word Recognition   T38   64
    Test 2: Reading Vocabulary   T39   67
    Test 3: Reading Comprehension   T40   69
    Test 4: Math Concepts   T41   76
    Test 5: Math Problems   T43   81
    Test 6: Math Procedures   T44   84
    Test 7: Language   T45   86

Answer Key   Inside Back Cover

© Steck-Vaughn Publishing Company   Primary 1 Intro, SV 7165-1

About the Program

Test Practice on the Metropolitan Achievement Tests has been developed to refresh basic skills, familiarize students with test formats and directions, and teach test-taking strategies for the Metropolitan Achievement Tests. *Test Practice* provides teachers with materials to ensure that students take the test under optimal conditions—that test-wise students be able to concentrate on what they know without being overwhelmed by a testing situation with which they are unfamiliar.

Being well prepared for a test means knowing how to approach different types of questions and how to use time wisely. By using the *Test Practice* books prior to the administration of the Metropolitan Achievement Tests, students will learn such skills, as well as be able to control their anxiety about a test and to keep their concentration high throughout the testing period.

The Steck-Vaughn *Test Practice* Series for Grades 1–5

Test Practice on the Metropolitan Achievement Tests consists of five books. You will need to determine which book is best suited to the abilities and needs of your students. The series is organized as follows:

Book	Grade Level
Primary 1	Grade 1
Primary 2	Grade 2
Elementary 1	Grade 3
Elementary 2	Grade 4
Intermediate 1	Grade 5

Objectives of the Series

To Increase Awareness of Test-Taking Strategies

Test-taking strategies should focus on four important test principles:

1. Time Use
   - Not spending too much time on any one question
   - Working rapidly but comfortably
   - Marking items to return to if time permits
   - Using any time remaining to review answers
   - Using a watch (at the appropriate age) to keep track of time
2. Error Avoidance
   - Paying careful attention to directions
   - Determining clearly what is being asked
   - Marking answers in the appropriate place
   - Checking all answers if time permits
   - Being neat by avoiding making stray marks on the test
3. Reasoning
   - Reading the entire question or passage and all the choices before answering a question
   - Applying what has been learned
4. Guessing
   - Answering all the questions in the test within the allotted time—remember: there is no penalty for guessing on the Metropolitan Achievement Tests.
   - Trying to eliminate known incorrect answer choices before guessing

To Increase Awareness of Directions

It is important that students understand the directions for taking the tests. Therefore, one of the key objectives of the program is to familiarize students with directions. Doing so builds self-confidence and permits students to utilize their time more effectively.

To Increase Awareness of Content and Skills

Anxiety often results from a lack of information about the knowledge and skills the tests will cover. You and your students will find that increased awareness of content and skills are significant outcomes of the program.

To Increase Awareness of Format

By practicing the skills needed to meet your school's educational objectives, the students will gain invaluable experience with test formats. Such familiarity permits students to spend more time applying what they have learned.

To Understand How the Test Is Administered

Students are sometimes uncomfortable anticipating what will happen on the day of the tests. Becoming familiar with the procedures, directions, and the process of test taking helps reduce anxiety and uncertainty.

Format of the Books

Each of the five books is divided into units that correspond to those found in the Metropolitan Achievement Tests. The units vary but can include Prereading, Word Recognition, Reading Vocabulary, Reading Comprehension, Math Concepts, Math Problems, Math Procedures, and Language. Within each of these units are the skills covered on the tests.

Each skill lesson generally includes:

<u>Directions</u>—clear, concise, and similar to those found in the Metropolitan Achievement Tests;

<u>Try This</u>—A skill strategy for students that enables them to approach each lesson exercise in a logical manner;

A <u>Sample</u>—to familiarize students with test-taking items;

<u>Think It Through</u>—a specific explanation to students of the correct answer in the <u>Sample</u> item that tells why the correct answer is correct and why the incorrect answers are wrong;

A <u>Practice Section</u>—a set of exercises based on the lesson and modeled on the kinds of test items found in the Metropolitan Achievement Tests.

Each unit is followed by a <u>Unit Test</u> that covers all the skills in the unit lessons and affords students the opportunity to experience a situation close to the testing situation. Each book concludes with a series of <u>Comprehensive Tests</u>—one for each unit in the book. The Comprehensive Tests give students an opportunity to take a test under conditions that parallel those they will face when taking the Metropolitan Achievement Tests.

The Teacher's Section

The teacher's section of *Test Practice on the Metropolitan Achievement Tests* contains a Scope and Sequence. This teacher's section also provides a detailed plan of action and suggestions for teaching and administering each of the lessons and tests, including <u>Sample</u> items. Scripts are provided so that students become familiar with oral directions given on the tests themselves.

Also contained in this teacher's section is an introductory lesson designed to acquaint students with the *Test Practice on the Metropolitan Achievement Tests* program.

Scope and Sequence

READING SKILLS

Skill	Unit 1: Word Recognition	Lesson 1: Recognizing Beginning Sounds	Lesson 2: Recognizing Ending Sounds	Lesson 3: Recognizing Vowel Sounds	Unit 1 Test	Unit 2: Reading Vocabulary	Lesson 4: Matching Words with Similar Meanings	Lesson 5: Matching Words with Opposite Meanings	Unit 2 Test	Unit 3: Reading Comprehension	Lesson 6: Understanding Sentences	Lesson 7: Reading Stories	Unit 3 Test	COMPREHENSIVE TESTS 1, 2, 3
Recognizing and matching initial consonant sounds using pictures		■			■									■
Recognizing and matching final consonant sounds using pictures			■		■									■
Recognizing and matching vowel sounds				■	■									■
Identifying synonyms for words presented in context							■		■					■
Identifying antonyms for words presented in context								■	■					■
Comprehending simple sentences											■		■	■
Understanding stated details, actions, and reasons												■	■	■
Understanding sequences												■	■	■
Inferring ideas												■	■	■
Drawing conclusions												■	■	■
Understanding and interpreting ideas, events, and relationships												■	■	■
Evaluating and analyzing what is read												■	■	■

MATHEMATICS SKILLS

Skill	Unit 4: Math Concepts	Lesson 8: Working with Numeration	Lesson 9: Understanding Patterns and Relationships	Lesson 10: Working with Measurement	Lesson 11: Working with Geometry	Unit 4 Test	Unit 5: Math Problems	Lesson 12: Working with Number Sentences	Lesson 13: Solving Problems	Lesson 14: Working with Statistics and Probability	Unit 5 Test	Unit 6: Math Procedures	Lesson 15: Using Computation	Lesson 16: Using Computation in Word Problems	Unit 6 Test	COMPREHENSIVE TESTS 4, 5, 6
Recognizing names for numbers		■				■										■
Counting		■				■										■
Interpreting numbers from pictures		■				■										■
Comparing and ordering numbers		■				■										■
Understanding fractional parts			■			■										■
Interpreting number patterns			■			■										■
Understanding basic addition and subtraction operations			■			■										■
Determining the value of a group of coins				■		■										■
Using standard and nonstandard units to estimate length				■		■										■
Using a calendar to locate information				■		■										■
Telling time				■		■										■
Understanding geometric principles of size, shape, and symmetry					■	■										■
Identifying plane and solid figures					■	■										■
Recognizing properties of plane figures					■	■										■
Identifying patterns of geometric shapes					■	■										■
Identifying and reading number sentences								■	■							■
Using number sentences to solve problems								■	■							■
Identifying number sentences that represent pictures								■	■							■
Using problem-solving strategies to solve one-step and multiple-step word problems									■	■						■
Classifying geometric figures									■							■
Reading and interpreting picture graphs										■	■					■
Determining simple probability										■	■					■
Applying addition and subtraction to word problems													■	■	■	■
Adding and subtracting whole numbers with and without regrouping													■	■	■	■

Scope and Sequence

LANGUAGE SKILLS

	Unit 7: Language	Lesson 17: Building Listening Skills	Lesson 18: Prewriting, Composing, and Editing	Lesson 19: Finding Misspelled Words	Unit 7 Test	COMPREHENSIVE TEST 7
Listening to remember stated details, sequences, and directions		■			■	■
Drawing conclusions		■			■	■
Making inferences		■			■	■
Matching pictures that rhyme with words to complete poems		■			■	■
Distinguishing between reality and fantasy		■			■	■
Determining the purpose for writing			■		■	■
Determining appropriate topics			■		■	■
Organizing information and ideas			■		■	■
Determining topic relevance			■		■	■
Alphabetizing words			■		■	■
Using the parts of a book to locate information			■		■	■
Determining correct sentence order			■		■	■
Identifying extraneous information in paragraphs			■		■	■
Identifying correctly applied grammar			■		■	■
Identifying correct capitalization and punctuation			■		■	■
Identifying correctly and effectively written sentences			■		■	■
Identifying misspelled words in the context of dictated sentences				■	■	■
Recognizing the misspelling of sight words				■	■	■

© Steck-Vaughn Publishing Company

Introducing Students to *Test Practice*

Use this orientation lesson to familiarize students with the format of *Test Practice on the Metropolitan Achievement Tests*, Primer level, and with steps for preparing for and taking the Metropolitan Achievement Tests. Before you use this introduction to *Test Practice*, you need to make place markers for the students. Students will use the markers to help keep their place on the page. The place markers can be made of cardboard. They should be rectangles that measure about 4 inches by 2 inches.

SAY: **At certain times during the school year, you may take one or more special tests. These tests show how well you are doing in certain subjects, compared with other students of your age group across the country. Some test questions will be harder than others, and some may be new to you. But that's all right. You will be given enough time to work on each test.**

Distribute the *Test Practice* pages to students. Tell students that *Test Practice* will use the same kinds of questions that are on the special test, the Metropolitan Achievement Tests. Using the pages will be practice for taking the special test. Allow students to skim through the pages for a minute or two. Circulate around the room, making sure that all students are turned to the correct page as you examine the pages.

OPTIONAL: An introduction to the Unit Tests follows. If you prefer not to use them now, select the units and/or lessons with which your students need practice.

SAY: **Now we will look at one of the lessons. Start at the beginning of the page and turn to Unit 3 on page 11. Notice that this page has *Unit 3, Reading Comprehension*, at the top of the page. This tells you the number and the name of the unit. This unit is about reading. Just under the unit number and name it has *Lesson 6: Understanding Sentences*. That tells you the number and the name of the lesson. This lesson is about sentences. This is how a lesson page looks. What do you see just below the lesson number and name? (Another word) This is the word *Sample*. Sample tells you that this is a practice question. We will always work the samples together. What do you see in the same row with the Sample? (A picture) What do you see next to the picture? (Three circles and three sentences) These sentences are the answer choices. When you decide on your answer, you will use your pencil to darken the circle, or answer space, next to the correct answer choice. Let me show you how to darken the answer space.**

Draw a small circle on the chalkboard. Demonstrate the proper way to darken the answer space. Explain to students the importance of filling the answer space, pressing firmly with the pencil to make a dark mark, and erasing any stray marks that might be picked up as answers by the scoring machines. Ask students if they have any questions.

SAY: **What do you see at the right, at the end of the row for the Sample? (A stop sign) What should you do when you see a stop sign? (Stop what you are doing.)**

Tell students that they will see stop signs throughout the lessons and on the Metropolitan Achievement Tests. Explain that the stop sign is used to tell students to stop what they are doing, put their pencils down, and wait for further instructions from the teacher.

SAY: **Now look directly below the row for the Sample. What do you see? (The numbers *1, 2, 3, 4* and more pictures, answer circles, and sentences) The numbers at the beginning of each row stand for the lesson questions. The sentences stand for the answer choices. I will ask you questions, and you will look at the answer choices. Then you will choose your answer.**

Distribute the place markers to students.

SAY: **This is a marker. You will use it to help you keep your place on the page. It will help to make sure that you are working on the correct item.**

Demonstrate by placing a marker just under the answer circles in the Sample. Circulate around the classroom, making sure that all students see the correct placement of the marker.

SAY: **Now see if you can place your marker under the next row, the one with the picture of the man and the number *1*.**

Check to see that all students have placed their markers correctly. Ask students if they have any questions about the lesson page.

SAY: **Now turn to page 12. You should be on the page with *Lesson 7: Reading Stories* at the top of the page. This is the next lesson in Unit 3. This lesson is about stories.**

Make sure that all students find page 12. Explain that most units have more than one lesson.

SAY: **Now look at the bottom of page 12. What do you see at the right, just below question 4? (An arrow with the words *GO ON*). This tells you to go to the next page.**

Tell students that in some lessons and in other places in the *Test Practice* book they will see the arrow with the words *GO ON*. Ask students if they have any questions.

SAY: **Now turn to page 18. You should be on the page with Unit 3 Test at the top of the page.**

Make sure that all students find page 18. Explain that there is a unit test at the end of each unit that gives students an opportunity to practice taking a test.

Tell students to look at page 18. Have students locate Sample A on the test. Tell students that you will always work the samples together as a class. Explain that the unit test will include the skills you have practiced together in the unit lessons.

SAY: **Now look at the bottom of page 18. What do you see at the right, just below the last row of pictures? (A stop sign) What does the stop sign tell you to do? (Stop what you are doing, put your pencils down, and wait for further instructions from the teacher.)**

Ask students if they have any questions about the unit tests.

UNIT 1 Word Recognition

Lesson 1: Recognizing Beginning Sounds

Reading Skills: Recognizing and matching initial consonant sounds using pictures

SAY: **Turn to Lesson 1, Recognizing Beginning Sounds, on page 1.**

Check to see that all students find Lesson 1. Introduce the Try This feature.

SAY: **In Lesson 1 you will practice finding words that begin with the same sounds as pictures.**

Listen carefully. When you look at the picture, you should try this: listen to the beginning sound of the name of the picture. Remember that sound. Then find the word that begins with the same sound.

Place your marker under the first row, the one with the picture of the mask. This is the Sample. Now look at the words next to the picture. Darken the circle for the word that begins with the same sound as mask...mask.

Allow students time to choose and mark their answer. Remind students to carefully fill in the answer space and to completely erase any stray marks. Then introduce the Think It Through feature.

SAY: **Now we will think it through. We will check the answer. You should have darkened the circle for the third word, *mountain*. The "m" in *mountain* makes the same sound as the "m" in *mask*. *Name* is not the correct answer because *name* has the "m" sound at the end of the word. *Know* and *your* are not correct because they do not have the "m" sound.**

Check to see that all students have filled in the correct answer space. If students have not filled in the correct answer space, caution them to completely erase their incorrect answer and to erase any stray marks before they darken the correct space. Remind students that they were instructed to find the word that begins with the same sound as the picture.

Ask students if they have any questions about the Sample or about darkening the answer space.

SAY: **Now you will practice finding more words that begin with the same sounds as pictures. Look carefully at the picture. Then choose your answer from the words given in the row.**

Now we will begin. Place your marker under the next row, the one with the picture of the basket.

Check to see that all students find item 1. Allow students time after each item to choose and mark their answer.

SAY: 1 **Look at the picture of the basket. Darken the circle for the word that begins with the same sound as *basket...basket*.**
2 **Place your marker under the next row. Look at the picture of the wheel. Darken the circle for the word that begins with the same sounds as *wheel...wheel*.**
3 **Place your marker under the next row. Look at the picture of the snowman. Darken the circle for the word that begins with the same sounds as *snowman...snowman*.**
4 **Place your marker under the next row. Look at the picture of the woman stirring something. Darken the circle for the word that begins with the same sounds as *stir...stir*.**
5 **Place your marker under the next row. Look at the picture of the closet. Darken the circle for the word that begins with the same sounds as *closet...closet*.**

Look at the stop sign at the bottom of the page. You have now finished the lesson and should put your pencils down.

Review the questions and answer choices with students. Discuss with the class why one answer is correct and the others are not correct. Also check to see that students have carefully filled in their answer spaces and have completely erased any stray marks.

Lesson 2: Recognizing Ending Sounds

Reading Skills: Recognizing and matching final consonant sounds using pictures

SAY: **Turn to Lesson 2, Recognizing Ending Sounds, on page 2.**

Check to see that all students find Lesson 2. Introduce the Try This feature.

SAY: **In Lesson 2 you will practice finding words that end with the same sounds as pictures.**

Listen carefully. When you look at the picture, you should try this: listen to the end sound of the name of the picture. Remember that sound. Then find the word that ends with the same sound.

Place your marker under the first row, the one with the picture of the game. This is the Sample. Now look at the words next to the picture. Darken the circle for the word that ends with the same sound as game...game.

Allow students time to choose and mark their answer. Remind students to carefully fill in the answer space and to completely erase any stray marks. Then introduce the Think It Through feature.

SAY: **Now we will think it through. We will check the answer. You should have darkened the circle for the last word, home. The "m" in home makes the same sound as the "m" in game. Monkey is not correct because monkey has the "m" sound at the beginning of the word. Ten and yellow are not correct because ten and yellow do not have an "m" sound.**

Check to see that all students have filled in the correct answer space. If students have not filled in the correct answer space, caution them to completely erase their incorrect answer and to erase any stray marks before they darken the correct space. Remind students that they were instructed to find the word that ends with the same sound as the picture.

Ask students if they have any questions about the Sample or about darkening the answer space.

SAY: **Now you will practice finding more words that end with the same sounds as pictures. Look carefully at each picture. Then choose your answer from the words given in the row.**

Now we will begin. Place your marker under the next row, the one with the picture of the boot.

Check to see that all students find item 1. Allow students time after each item to choose and mark their answer.

SAY: 1 **Look at the picture of the boot. Darken the circle for the word that ends with the same sound as boot...boot.**
2 **Place your marker under the next row. Look at the picture of the worm. Darken the circle for the word that ends with the same sounds as worm...worm.**
3 **Place your marker under the next row. Look at the picture of the boy washing dishes. Darken the circle for the word that ends with the same sounds as wash...wash.**
4 **Place your marker under the next row. Look at the picture of the girl jumping rope. Darken the circle for the word that ends with the same sounds as jump...jump.**
5 **Place your marker under the next row. Look at the picture of the skunk. Darken the circle for the word that ends with the same sounds as skunk...skunk.**

Look at the stop sign at the bottom of the page. You have now finished the lesson and should put your pencils down.

Review the questions and answer choices with students. Discuss with the class why one answer is correct and the others are not correct. Also check to see that students have carefully filled in their answer spaces and have completely erased any stray marks.

Lesson 3: Recognizing Vowel Sounds

Reading Skills: Recognizing and matching vowel sounds

SAY: **Turn to Lesson 3, Recognizing Vowel Sounds, on page 3.**

Check to see that all students find Lesson 3. Introduce the Try This feature.

SAY: **In Lesson 3 you will practice choosing words that have the same sound as underlined letters in words.**

Listen carefully. When you look at a word with an underlined letter, you should try

this: say the sound of the letter to yourself. Think about the sound. Then find the word that has the same sound.

Place your marker under the first row, the one with the word *time*. This is the Sample. Look at the underlined letter in *time*. Darken the circle for the word that has the same sound as the underlined letter in *time...time*.

Allow students time to choose and mark their answer. Remind students to carefully fill in the answer space and to completely erase any stray marks. Then introduce the Think It Through feature.

SAY: **Now we will think it through. We will check the answer. You should have darkened the circle for the third word, *shine*. *Shine* has the same sound as the underlined "i" in *time*.**

Check to see that all students have filled in the correct answer space. If students have not filled in the correct answer space, caution them to completely erase their incorrect answer and to erase any stray marks before they darken the correct space. Remind students that they were instructed to find the word with the same sound as an underlined letter.

Ask students if they have any questions about the Sample or about darkening the answer space.

SAY: **Now you will practice choosing more words that have the same sound as underlined letters in words. Put your marker under the next row, the one with the word *later*. Do numbers 1 through 9 just as we did the Sample. Look carefully at the underlined letter. Then choose your answer from the words given in the row. When you come to the stop sign at the bottom of the page, put your pencils down.**

Allow students time to choose and mark their answers.

Review the questions and answer choices with students. Discuss with the class why one answer is correct and the others are not correct. Also check to see that students have carefully filled in their answer spaces and have completely erased any stray marks.

UNIT 1 Test

SAY: **Turn to the Unit 1 Test on page 4.**

Check to see that all students find the Unit 1 Test.

SAY: **In the first part of this test, you will find words that begin with the same sounds as pictures. Place your marker under the first row, the one with the picture of the fan. This is Sample A. Now look at the words next to the picture. Darken the circle for the word that begins with the same sound as *fan...fan*.**

Allow students time to choose and mark their answer. Remind students that they were instructed to find the word that begins with the same sound as the picture *fan*.

SAY: **You should have darkened the circle for the first word, *fall*. The "f" in *fall* makes the same sound as the "f" in *fan*. *Half* is not correct because the "f" sound in *half* is at the end of the word. *Never* and *every* are not correct because they do not have an "f" sound.**

Check to see that all students have filled in the correct answer space. Ask students if they have any questions.

SAY: **Now you will find more words that begin with the same sounds as pictures. Look carefully at the picture. Then choose your answer from the words given in the row.**

Now we will begin. Place your marker under the next row, the one with the picture of the drum.

Check to see that all students find item 1. Allow students time after each item to choose and mark their answer.

SAY: 1 **Look at the picture of the drum. Darken the circle for the word that begins with the same sounds as *drum...drum*.**
2 **Place your marker under the next row. Look at the picture of the boy at the supermarket. Darken the circle for the word that begins with the same sounds as *shop...shop*.**
3 **Place your marker under the next row. Look at the picture of the cricket. Darken the circle for the word that begins with the same sounds as *cricket...cricket*.**
4 **Place your marker under the next row. Look at the picture of the jacket. Darken the circle for the word that begins with the same sound as *jacket...jacket*.**
5 **Place your marker under the next row. Look at the picture of the chair. Darken the circle for the word that begins with the same sounds as *chair...chair*.**

Look at the stop sign at the bottom of the page. You have finished this part of the test and should put your pencils down.

SAY: **Now look at the top of page 5.**

Check to see that all students find page 5.

SAY: **In the next part of the test, you will find words that end with the same sounds as pictures. Place your marker under the first row, the one with the picture of the jeep. This is <u>Sample B</u>. Now look at the words next to the picture. Darken the circle for the word that ends with the same sound as jeep...jeep.**

Allow students time to choose and mark their answer. Remind students that they were instructed to find the word that ends with the same sound as the picture jeep.

SAY: **You should have darkened the circle for the last word, clap. The "p" in clap makes the same sound as the "p" in jeep. School and touch are not correct because they do not have a "p" sound. Path is not correct because the "p" sound in path is at the beginning of the word.**

Check to see that all students have filled in the correct answer space. Ask students if they have any questions.

SAY: **Now you will find more words that end with the same sounds as pictures. Look carefully at the picture. Then choose your answer from the words given in the row.**

Now we will begin. Place your marker under the next row, the one with the picture of the leaf.

Check to see that all students find item 6. Allow students time after each item to choose and mark their answer.

SAY: 6 **Look at the picture of the leaf. Darken the circle for the word that ends with the same sound as leaf...leaf.**
 7 **Place your marker under the next row. Look at the picture of the teeth. Darken the circle for the word that ends with the same sounds as teeth...teeth.**
 8 **Place your marker under the next row. Look at the picture of the sink. Darken the circle for the word that ends with the same sounds as sink...sink.**
 9 **Place your marker under the next row. Look at the picture of the block. Darken the circle for the word that ends with the same sounds as block...block.**
 10 **Place your marker under the next row. Look at the picture of the yard. Darken the circle for the word that ends with the same sounds as yard...yard.**

Look at the stop sign at the bottom of the page. You have finished this part of the test and should put your pencils down.

SAY: **Now turn to page 6.**

Check to see that all students find page 6.

SAY: **In the last part of the test, you will choose words that have the same sound as underlined letters in words. Place your marker under the first row, the one with the word bean. This is <u>Sample C</u>. Look at the underlined letters in bean. Darken the circle for the word that has the same sound as the underlined letters in bean...bean.**

Allow students time to choose and mark their answer.

SAY: **You should have darkened the circle for the last word, leak. Leak has the same sound as the underlined "ea" in the word bean.**

Check to see that all students have filled in the correct answer space. Ask students if they have any questions.

SAY: **Now you will choose more words that have the same sound as underlined letters in words. Put your marker under the next row, the one with the word plate. Do numbers 11 through 19 just as we did <u>Sample C</u>. Look carefully at the underlined letter. Then choose your answer from the words given in the row. When you come to the stop sign at the bottom of the page, put your pencils down.**

Allow students time to choose and mark their answers.

SAY: **You have completed the Unit 1 Test. Make sure that you have carefully filled in your answer spaces and have erased any stray marks. Then put your pencils down.**

After the test has been scored, review the questions and answer choices with students. If students are having difficulty, provide them with additional practice.

UNIT 2 Reading Vocabulary

Lesson 4: Matching Words with Similar Meanings

Reading Skill: Identifying synonyms for words presented in context

SAY: **Turn to Lesson 4, Matching Words with Similar Meanings, on page 7.**

Check to see that all students find Lesson 4. Introduce the Try This feature.

SAY: **In Lesson 4 you will practice finding words that have the same or almost the same meaning as underlined words in sentences.**

Listen carefully. When you read a sentence you should try this: look at the underlined word. Think what that word means. Then read the answer choices. Find the word that means the same or almost the same as the underlined word. Place your marker under the first sentence. This is the Sample. *Put the flowers on the table.* **Now read the four words listed below the sentence:** *Hold, Place, See, Take.* **Darken the circle next to the word that means the same or almost the same as** *Put.*

Allow students time to choose and mark their answer. Then introduce the Think It Through feature.

SAY: **Now we will think it through. We will check the answer. You should have darkened the circle next to the second word,** *Place. Place* **means the same as** *Put. Hold, See,* **and** *Take* **are not correct because they do not mean the same as** *Put.*

Check to see that all students have filled in the correct answer space. Ask students if they have any questions.

SAY: **Now you will practice finding more words that mean the same or almost the same as underlined words in sentences. Do numbers 1 through 7 just as we did the Sample. When you come to the stop sign at the bottom of the page, put your pencils down. You may now begin.**

Review the questions and answer choices with students. Discuss with the class why one answer is correct and the others are not correct. Also check to see that students have carefully filled in their answer spaces and have completely erased any stray marks.

© Steck-Vaughn Publishing Company

Lesson 5: Matching Words with Opposite Meanings

Reading Skill: Identifying antonyms for words presented in context

SAY: **Turn to Lesson 5, Matching Words with Opposite Meanings, on page 8.**

Check to see that all students find Lesson 5. Introduce the Try This feature.

SAY: **In Lesson 5 you will practice finding words with meanings that are the opposite of underlined words in sentences.**

Listen carefully. When you read a sentence you should try this: look at the underlined word. Think what that word means. Then read the answer choices. Find the word that means the opposite or almost the opposite of the underlined word. Place your marker under the first sentence. This is the Sample. Read the sentence silently as I read it aloud. *Please close the back door.* **Now read the four words listed below the sentence:** *front, center, broken, closet.* **Darken the circle next to the word that means the opposite or almost the opposite of** *back.*

Allow students time to choose and mark their answer. Then introduce the Think It Through feature.

SAY: **Now we will think it through. We will check the answer. You should have darkened the circle next to the first word,** *front. Front* **means the opposite of** *back. Center, broken,* **and** *closet* **are not correct because they do not mean the opposite of** *back.*

Check to see that all students have filled in the correct answer space. Ask students if they have any questions.

SAY: **Now you will practice finding more words that mean the opposite or almost the opposite of underlined words in sentences. Do numbers 1 through 7 just as we did the Sample. When you come to the stop sign at the bottom of the page, put your pencils down. You may now begin.**

Review the questions and answer choices with students. Discuss with the class why one answer is correct and the others are not correct. Also check to see that students have carefully filled in their answer spaces and have completely erased any stray marks.

UNIT 2 Test

SAY: **Turn to the Unit 2 Test on page 9.**

Check to see that all students find the Unit 2 Test.

SAY: **In the first part of the test, you will find words that have the same or almost the same meaning as underlined words in sentences. Place your marker under the first sentence. This is Sample A. Read the sentence silently as I read it aloud.** *Don't hurt yourself.* **Now read the four words listed below the sentence:** *help, scare, harm, lose.* **Darken the circle next to the word that means the same or almost the same as** *hurt.*

Allow students time to choose and mark their answer.

SAY: **You should have darkened the circle next to the third word,** *harm. Harm* **means the same as** *hurt. Help, scare,* **and** *lose* **are not correct because they do not mean the same as** *hurt.*

Check to see that all students have filled in the correct answer space. Ask students if they have any questions.

SAY: **Now you will find more words that mean the same or almost the same as underlined words in sentences. Place your marker under the next sentence. Do numbers 1 through 7 just as we did Sample A. Read each sentence and the four words listed. Then darken the circle next to the word that means the same or almost the same as the underlined word. When you come to the stop sign at the bottom of the page, put your pencils down. You may now begin.**

Review the questions and answer choices with students. Discuss with the class why one answer is correct and the others are not correct. Also check to see that students have carefully filled in their answer spaces and have completely erased any stray marks.

SAY: **Now turn to page 10.**

Check to see that all students find page 10.

SAY: **In the next part of the test, you will find words with meanings that are the opposite or almost the opposite of underlined words in sentences. Place your marker under the first sentence. This is Sample B. Read the sentence silently as I read it aloud.** *Do you need more money?* **Now read the four words listed below the sentence:** *some, less, any, my.* **Darken the circle next to the word that means the opposite or almost the opposite of** *more.*

Allow students time to choose and mark their answer.

SAY: **You should have darkened the circle next to the second word,** *less. Less* **means the opposite of** *more. Some, any,* **and** *my* **are not correct because they do not mean the opposite of** *more.*

Check to see that all students have filled in the correct answer space. Ask students if they have any questions.

SAY: **Now you will find more words that mean the opposite or almost the opposite of underlined words in sentences. Place your marker under the next sentence. Do numbers 8 through 14 just as we did Sample B. Read each sentence and the four words listed. Then darken the circle next to the word that means the opposite or almost the opposite of the underlined word. When you come to the stop sign at the bottom of the page, put your pencils down. You may now begin.**

Allow students time to choose and mark their answers.

SAY: **It is now time to stop. You have completed the Unit 2 Test. Make sure that you have carefully filled in your answer spaces and have completely erased any stray marks. Then put your pencils down.**

After the test has been scored, review the questions and answer choices with students. If students are having difficulty, provide them with additional practice.

UNIT 3 Reading Comprehension

Lesson 6: Understanding Sentences

Reading Skill: Comprehending simple sentences

SAY: **Turn to Lesson 6, Understanding Sentences, on page 11.**

Check to see that all students find Lesson 6. Introduce the Try This feature.

SAY: **In Lesson 6 you will practice finding sentences that tell about pictures. Listen carefully. When you look at the picture, you should try this: look at what is happening in the picture. Then read each sentence. Find the sentence that tells what is happening in the picture. Place your marker under the picture in the first row. This is the Sample. Now look at the sentences next to the picture. Darken the circle next to the sentence that tells what is happening in the picture.**

Allow students time to choose and mark their answer.

T12 © Steck-Vaughn Publishing Company

Primary 1 Intro, SV 7165-1

Then introduce the Think It Through feature.

SAY: **Now we will think it through. We will check the answer. You should have darkened the circle next to the second sentence. This sentence tells what is happening in the picture.**

Check to see that all students have filled in the correct answer space. Ask students if they have any questions about the Sample or about darkening the answer space.

SAY: **Now you will practice finding more sentences that tell about pictures. Place your marker under the next picture. Do numbers 1 through 4 just as we did the Sample. Darken the circle next to the sentence that tells what is happening in the picture. When you come to the stop sign at the bottom of the page, put your pencils down. You may now begin.**

Allow students time to choose and mark their answers.

Review the questions and answer choices with students. Discuss with the class why one answer is correct and the others are not correct. Also check to see that students have carefully filled in their answer spaces and have completely erased any stray marks.

Lesson 7: Reading Stories

Reading Skills: Understanding stated details, actions, and reasons; understanding sequences; inferring ideas; drawing conclusions; understanding and interpreting ideas, events, and relationships; evaluating and analyzing what is read

SAY: **Turn to Lesson 7, Reading Stories, on page 12.**

Check to see that all students find Lesson 7. Introduce the Try This feature.

SAY: **In Lesson 7 you will practice answering questions about stories that you read.**

Listen carefully. After you read a story, you should try this: carefully read the questions and the answer choices. More than one answer choice may seem correct. Be sure to find the answer that goes best with the story.

Place your marker under the first row, the one that has the title, *Our Toys*. This is the Sample. Read the story. Then read the question and the answer choices. Darken the circle next to the correct answer.

Allow students time to choose and mark their answer. Remind students to carefully fill in the answer circle and to completely erase any stray marks. Then introduce the Think It Through feature.

SAY: **Now we will think it through. We will check the answer. You should have darkened the circle next to the second answer choice. The third sentence in the story tells you that Ron's car is *blue*. It is not red or yellow. The correct answer is the second answer choice.**

Check to see that all students have filled in the correct answer space. Remind students that they were instructed to find the answer that best goes with the story.

Ask students if they have any questions about the Sample or about darkening the answer circle.

SAY: **Now you will practice answering more questions about stories that you read. Place your marker under the next row, the one that has the title, *What did Danny learn*? Do numbers 1 through 22 just as we did the Sample. Read each story. Then read the questions and the answer choices that follow. Darken the circle next to the correct answer. When you come to the arrow at the bottom of the page, continue working on the next page. When you come to the stop sign at the bottom of page 17, put your pencils down. You may now begin.**

Allow students time to choose and mark their answers.

Review the questions and answer choices with students. Discuss with the class why one answer is correct and the others are not correct. Also check to see that students have carefully filled in their answer spaces and have completely erased any stray marks.

UNIT 3 Test

SAY: **Turn to the Unit 3 Test on page 18.**

Check to see that all students find the Unit 3 Test.

SAY: **In the first part of the test, you will find sentences that tell about pictures. Place your marker under the picture in the first row. This is Sample A. Now look at the sentences next to the picture. Darken the circle next to the sentence that tells what is happening in the picture.**

Allow students time to choose and mark their answer.

SAY: **You should have darkened the circle next to the first sentence, *The girl is watching a bird*. This sentence tells what is happening in the picture. The second sentence is not correct because it is not raining in the picture. The third sentence is not correct because the picture does not show the girl planting flowers. Only the first sentence tells about the picture.**

Check to see that all students have filled in the correct answer space. Ask students if they have any questions.

SAY: **Now you will practice finding more sentences that tell about pictures. Place your marker under the picture in the next row. Do numbers 1 through 4 just as we did Sample A. Look at each picture. Then read the sentences next to the picture. Darken the circle next to the sentence that tells what is happening in the picture. When you come to the stop sign at the bottom of the page, put your pencils down. You may now begin.**

Allow students time to choose and mark their answers.

SAY: **Now turn to page 19.**

Check to see that all students find page 19.

SAY: **In the last part of the test, you will answer questions about stories that you read. Place your marker under the first row, the one that has the title, Playing. This is Sample B. Read the story. Then read the questions and the answer choices. Darken the circle next to the correct answer.**

Allow students time to choose and mark their answer.

SAY: **You should have darkened the circle next to the second answer choice, Sue Lin. The second sentence in the story tells you that Sue Lin is the child who hits the ball. The first answer choice is not correct because Max is not the child who hits the ball. The third answer choice is not correct because James is not the child who hits the ball. The correct answer is the second answer choice.**

Check to see that all students have filled in the correct answer space. Ask students if they have any questions.

SAY: **Now you will practice answering more questions about stories that you read. Place your marker under the next row, the one that has the title, Rosa's Good Deed. Do numbers 1 through 22 just as we did Sample B. Read each story. Then read the questions and the answer choices that follow. Darken the circle next to the correct answer. When you come to the arrow at the bottom of the page, continue working on the next page. When you come to the stop sign at the bottom of page 24, put your pencils down. You may now begin.**

Allow students time to choose and mark their answers.

SAY: **It is now time to stop. You have finished the Unit 3 Test. Make sure that you have carefully filled in your answer spaces and have completely erased any stray marks. Then put your pencils down.**

Review the questions and answer choices with students. Discuss with the class why one answer is correct and the others are not correct. Also check to see that students have carefully filled in their answer spaces and have completely erased any stray marks.

UNIT 4 Math Concepts

Lesson 8: Working with Numeration

Mathematics Skills: Recognizing names for numbers; counting; interpreting numbers from pictures; comparing and ordering numbers

SAY: **Turn to Lesson 8, Working with Numeration, on page 25.**

Check to see that all students find Lesson 8. Introduce the Try This feature.

SAY: **In Lesson 8 you will practice choosing pictures and numbers that answer math problems about numbers.**

Listen carefully. When I read a problem, you should try this: look at each picture or number for the problem. Think carefully about the information in the problem. Then find the picture or number that answers the problem you hear.

Place your marker under the first row, the one with the picture of the birds. This is the Sample. Now listen carefully. Darken the circle for the number that tells *exactly how many birds are shown in the picture*.

Allow students time to choose and mark their answer. Remind students to carefully fill in the answer space and to completely erase any stray marks. Then introduce the Think it Through feature.

SAY: **Now we will think it through. We will check the answer. You should have darkened the circle for the second number, *8*. There are *eight birds* shown in the picture.**

Check to see that all students have filled in the correct answer space. If students have not filled in the correct answer space, caution them to completely erase their incorrect answer and to erase any stray marks before they darken the correct space. Remind students that they were instructed to choose the number that tells how many birds are shown in the picture.

Ask students if they have any questions about the Sample or about darkening the answer space.

T14   © Steck-Vaughn Publishing Company   Primary 1 Intro, SV 7165-1

SAY: **Now you will practice choosing more pictures and numbers that answer math problems about numbers. Listen carefully to each problem. Then choose your answer from the pictures or numbers given for the problem.**

Now we will begin. Place your marker under the next row. Look at the picture of the bowl and the apples.

Check to see that all students find item 1. Allow students time after each item to choose and mark their answer. Do not say the item numbers.

SAY: 1 **Darken the circle for *the apple that is seventh from the bowl...the apple that is seventh from the bowl*.**
2 **Place your marker under the next row, the one with the paper clips. Each circle has ten paper clips. There are also some extra paper clips. How many paper clips are there altogether? Darken the circle for *the number of paper clips altogether*.**
3 **Place your marker under the next row, the one with the numbers. Which numeral names the most number of things? Darken the circle for the numeral which names *the most number of things*.**
4 **Place your marker under the last row on the page. Look at the numbers. Which number is between forty-nine and sixty-seven in value? Darken the circle for the number that is *between forty-nine and sixty-seven in value*.**

Look at the stop sign at the bottom of the page. You have now finished the lesson and should put your pencils down.

Review the questions and answer choices with students. Discuss with the class why one answer is correct and the others are not correct. Also check to see that students have carefully filled in their answer spaces and have completely erased any stray marks.

Lesson 9: Understanding Patterns and Relationships

Mathematics Skills: Understanding fractional parts; interpreting number patterns; understanding basic addition and subtraction operations

SAY: **Turn to Lesson 9, Understanding Patterns and Relationships, on page 26.**

Check to see that all students find Lesson 9. Introduce the Try This feature.

SAY: **In Lesson 9 you will practice choosing pictures and numbers that answer math problems about numbers and patterns.**

Listen carefully. When I read a problem, you should try this: look at each picture or number for the problem. Think carefully about the information in the problem. Then find the picture or number that answers the problem you hear.

Place your marker under the first row, the one with the numbers in boxes. This is the Sample. Now listen carefully. These numbers are counted by threes. Which number belongs in the empty box? Darken the circle for the number that *belongs in the empty box*.

Allow students time to choose and mark their answer. Remind students to carefully fill in the answer space and to completely erase any stray marks. Then introduce the Think it Through feature.

SAY: **Now we will think it through. We will check the answer. You should have darkened the circle for the third number, *12*. When you count by threes, you count *three, six, nine, twelve,* and *fifteen*.**

Check to see that all students have filled in the correct answer space. If students have not filled in the correct answer space, caution them to completely erase their incorrect answer and to erase any stray marks before they darken the correct space. Remind students that they were instructed to choose the number that goes in the empty box. Ask students if they have any questions about the Sample or about darkening the answer space.

SAY: **Now you will practice choosing more pictures and numbers that answer math problems about numbers and patterns. Listen carefully to each problem. Then choose your answer from the pictures or numbers given for the problem.**

Now we will begin. Place your marker under the next row. Look at the pictures of the divided, shaded figures.

Check to see that all students find item 1. Allow students time after each item to choose and mark their answer. Do not say the item numbers.

SAY: 1 **Carefully look at each of the figures. Darken the circle for the figure that has *four-fifths shaded...four-fifths shaded*.**
2 **Place your marker under the next row, the one with the numbers in boxes. These numbers are counted by fives. Which number belongs in the empty box? Darken the circle for the number that *belongs in the empty box*.**
3 **Place your marker under the next row, the one with the number sentences. Which number sentence is in the same**

fact family as 3 + 5 = 8? Darken the circle for the number sentence that is *in the same fact family as 3 + 5 = 8*.

4   Place your marker under the last row on the page. Carefully look at each of the figures. Darken the circle for the figure that has *one-fourth shaded...one-fourth shaded*.

Look at the stop sign at the bottom of the page. You have now finished the lesson and should put your pencils down.

Review the questions and answer choices with students. Discuss with the class why one answer is correct and the others are not correct. Also check to see that students have carefully filled in their answer spaces and have completely erased any stray marks.

Lesson 10: Working with Measurement

Mathematics Skills: Determining the value of groups of coins; using standard and nonstandard units to estimate length; using a calendar to locate information; telling time

SAY: **Turn to Lesson 10, Working with Measurement, on page 27.**

Check to see that all students find Lesson 10. Introduce the Try This feature.

SAY: **In Lesson 10 you will practice choosing pictures and numbers that answer problems about measurement.**

Listen carefully. When I read a problem, you should try this: look at each picture or number for the problem. Think carefully about the information in the problem. Then find the picture or number that answers the problem you hear.

Place your marker under the first row, the one with the pictures of coins. This is the Sample. Now listen carefully. Darken the circle under the number that tells *the exact value of the coins*.

Allow students time to choose and mark their answer. Remind students to carefully fill in the answer space and to completely erase any stray marks. Then introduce the Think it Through feature.

SAY: **Now we will think it through. We will check the answer. You should have darkened the circle for the last amount, *21¢*. The correct answer is *twenty-one cents*. The dime, two nickels and the penny have a value of *twenty-one cents*.**

Check to see that all students have filled in the correct answer space. If students have not filled in the correct answer space, caution them to completely erase their incorrect answer and to erase any stray marks before they darken the correct space. Remind students that they were instructed to choose a number that tells the exact value of the coins.

Ask students if they have any questions about the Sample or about darkening the answer space.

SAY: **Now you will practice choosing more pictures and numbers that answer math problems about measurement. Listen carefully to each problem. Then choose your answer from the pictures or numbers given for the problem.**

Now we will begin. Place your marker under the next row. Look at the picture of the leaves and the rake.

Check to see that all students find item 1. Allow students time after each item to choose and mark their answer. Do not say the item numbers.

SAY: 1   **Be sure to move your marker so you can see all of the answer choices. Darken the circle for the number that tells *about how many leaves long the rake is*.**

2   **Place your marker under the next row, the one with the picture of the pencil and the ruler. Darken the circle for the number that tells *how long the pencil is*.**

3   **Place your marker under the next row, the one with the calendar for January. Darken the circle for the date of *the first Tuesday in January*.**

4   **Place your marker under the last row on the page. Look at the clocks. Darken the circle for the clock that shows *eight-thirty...eight-thirty*.**

Look at the arrow with the words *GO ON* at the bottom of the page. This tells you to go to the next page and continue working on the lesson.

SAY: **Now turn to page 28.**

Check to see that all students find page 28.

SAY: **Now we will continue the lesson. Place your marker under the first row, the one with the pictures of coins.**

Check to see that all students find item 5. Allow students time after each item to choose and mark their answer. Do not say the item numbers.

SAY: 5   **Darken the circle under the number that tells *the exact value of the coins*.**

6. Place your marker under the next row, the one with the picture of the nail and the ruler. Be sure to move your marker so you can see all of the answer choices. Darken the circle for the number that tells *how long the nail is.*

7. Place your marker under the next row, the one with the calendar. Darken the circle for the day of the week that is *August twenty-ninth.*

8. Place your marker under the next row, the one with the picture of the turtle and the ruler. Be sure to move your marker so you can see all of the answer choices. Darken the circle for the number that tells *about how many centimeters long the turtle is.*

9. Place your marker under the last row on the page. Look at the clocks. Darken the circle for the clock that shows *seven o'clock...seven o'clock.*

Look at the stop sign at the bottom of the page. You have now finished the lesson and should put your pencils down.

Review the questions and answer choices with students. Discuss with the class why one answer is correct and the others are not correct. Also check to see that students have carefully filled in their answer spaces and have completely erased any stray marks.

Lesson 11: Working with Geometry

Mathematics Skills: Understanding geometric principles of size, shape, and symmetry; identifying plane and solid figures; recognizing properties of plane figures; identifying patterns of geometric shapes

SAY: **Turn to Lesson 11, Working with Geometry, on page 29.**

Check to see that all students find Lesson 11. Introduce the Try This feature.

SAY: **In Lesson 11 you will practice choosing pictures and numbers that answer math problems about figures and shapes.**

Listen carefully. When I read a problem, you should try this: look at each picture or number for the problem. Think carefully about the information in the problem. Then find the picture or number that answers the problem you hear.

Place your marker under the first row, the one with the pictures of different shapes and figures. This is the Sample. Now listen carefully. Darken the circle under the set of shapes that shows *a square and a circle together...a square and a circle together.*

Allow students time to choose and mark their answer. Remind students to carefully fill in the answer space and to completely erase any stray marks. Then introduce the Think it Through feature.

SAY: **Now we will think it through. We will check the answer. You should have darkened the circle for the *last* set of shapes. The last set shows *a square with a circle under the square.***

Check to see that all students have filled in the correct answer space. If students have not filled in the correct answer space, caution them to completely erase their incorrect answer and to erase any stray marks before they darken the correct space. Remind students that they were instructed to choose a set of shapes that show a square and a circle together.

Ask students if they have any questions about the Sample or about darkening the answer space.

SAY: **Now you will practice choosing more pictures and numbers that answer math problems about figures and shapes. Listen carefully to each problem. Then choose your answer from the pictures or numbers given for the problem.**

Now we will begin. Place your marker under the next row. Look at the picture of the large shape at the beginning of the row.

Check to see that all students find item 1. Allow students time after each item to choose and mark their answer. Do not say the item numbers.

SAY: 1. **Darken the circle for the number that tells *how many corners there are on the figure.***

2. **Place your marker under the next row, the one with the picture of a folded piece of paper. A shape has been cut out of this folded piece of paper. Darken the circle for the picture that shows *the shape that was cut from the paper.***

3. **Place your marker under the next row, the one with the pattern of shapes. Be sure to move your marker so you can see the answer choices. Darken the circle for *the two shapes that come next in this pattern.***

4. **Place your marker under the last row on the page. Look at the four items. Darken the circle for the item that is *shaped like a cylinder... shaped like a cylinder.***

Look at the arrow with the words *GO ON* at the bottom of the page. This tells you to go to the next page and continue working on the lesson.

SAY: **Now turn to page 30.**

Check to see that all students find page 30.

SAY: **Now we will continue the lesson. Place your marker under the first row.**

Check to see that all students find item 5. Allow students time after each item to choose and mark their answer. Do not say the item numbers.

SAY: 5 Darken the circle for the item that is *shaped like a triangle...shaped like a triangle.*
 6 Place your marker under the next row, the one with the picture of the large figure. Darken the circle for the number that tells *how many corners are on this figure.*
 7 Place your marker under the next row, the one with the picture of a folded piece of paper. A shape has been cut out of this folded piece of paper. Darken the circle for the picture that shows *the shape that was cut from the paper.*
 8 Place your marker under the last row, the one with the pattern of shapes. Be sure to move your marker so you can see all the answer choices. Darken the circle for *the two shapes that come next in this pattern.*

Look at the stop sign at the bottom of the page. You have now finished the lesson and should put your pencils down.

Review the questions and answer choices with students. Discuss with the class why one answer is correct and the others are not correct. Also check to see that students have carefully filled in their answer spaces and have completely erased any stray marks.

UNIT 4 Test

SAY: **Turn to the Unit 4 Test on page 31.**

Check to see that all students find the Unit 4 Test.

SAY: **In this test you will choose pictures and numbers that answer math problems you hear. Place your marker under the first row, the one with the picture of rabbits. This is Sample A. Now listen carefully. Darken the circle for the number that tells *exactly how many rabbits are shown in the picture.***

Allow students time to choose and mark their answer. Remind students that they were instructed to find the number that tells exactly how many rabbits are shown in the picture.

SAY: **You should have darkened the circle for the third number, *8*. There are *eight* rabbits in the picture.**

Check to see that all students have filled in the correct answer space.

Ask students if they have any questions.

SAY: **Now place your marker on the next row, the one with the numbers. This is Sample B. Now listen carefully. Darken the circle for the number *twenty-five...twenty-five.***

Allow students time to choose and mark their answer. Remind students that they were instructed to find the number *twenty-five.*

SAY: **You should have darkened the circle for the first number. This is the number *twenty-five.***

Check to see that all students have filled in the correct answer space. Ask students if they have any questions.

SAY: **Now you will choose more pictures and numbers that answer math problems. Listen carefully to each problem. Then choose your answer from the pictures or numbers given in the row. Place your marker under the next row, the one with the fishbowl and the fish.**

Check to see that all students find item 1. Allow students time after each item to choose and mark their answer. Do not say the item numbers.

SAY: 1 Darken the circle for *the number that tells the position of the dark fish from the fishbowl.*
 2 Place your marker under the next row. Darken the circle for the number *sixty-four...sixty-four.*
 3 Place your marker under the last row, the one with the marbles. Each bag has ten marbles. There are also some extra marbles. How many marbles are there altogether? Darken the circle for *the number that tells how many marbles there are altogether.*

Look at the arrow with the words *GO ON* at the bottom of the page. This tells you to go to the next page and continue working on the test.

SAY: **Now turn to page 32.**

Check to see that all students find page 32.

SAY: **Now we will continue the test. Place your marker under the first row.**

Check to see that all students find item 4. Allow students time after each item to choose and mark their answer. Do not say the item numbers.

SAY: 4 **Which numeral names the least number of things? Darken the circle for the numeral which names *the least number of things.***
 5 Place your marker under the next row.

Which numeral names the most number of things? Darken the circle for the numeral which names *the most number of things.*

6. Place your marker under the next row on the page. Which number is between fifty-six and seventy-four in value? Darken the circle for the number *between fifty-six and seventy-four in value.*

7. Place your marker under the next row. Which number is between seventy-three and ninety-one in value? Darken the circle for the number *between seventy-three and ninety-one in value.*

8. Place your marker under the last row on the page, the one with the divided, shaded figures. Darken the circle for *the figure that has one-sixth shaded...the figure that has one-sixth shaded.*

Look at the arrow with the words *GO ON* at the bottom of the page. This tells you to go to the next page and continue working on the test.

SAY: **Now look at page 33.**

Check to see that all students find page 33.

SAY: **Now we will continue the test. Place your marker under the first row, the one with the numbers in boxes.**

Check to see that all students find item 9. Allow students time after each item to choose and mark their answer. Do not say the item numbers.

SAY:
9. These numbers are counted by fours. Which number belongs in the empty box? Darken the circle for the number that *belongs in the empty box.*
10. Place your marker under the next row, the one with the numbers in the boxes. These numbers are counted by threes. Which number belongs in the empty box? Darken the circle for the number that *belongs in the empty box.*
11. Place your marker under the next row, the one with the number sentences. Which number sentence is in the same fact family as 6 + 2 = 8? Darken the circle for the number sentence that is *in the same fact family as 6 + 2 = 8.*
12. Place your marker under the next row, the one with the pictures of the coins. Look at the coins carefully. Darken the circle under the number that tells *the exact value of the coins.*
13. Place your marker under the last row on the page. Look at the coins carefully. Darken the circle under the number that tells *the exact value of the coins.*

SAY: **Look at the arrow with the words GO ON at the bottom of the page. This tells you to go to the next page and continue working on the test.**

SAY: **Now turn to page 34.**

Check to see that all students find page 34.

SAY: **Now we will continue the test. Place your marker under the first row, the one with the picture of the chain and the ruler.**

Check to see that all students find item 14. Allow students time after each item to choose and mark their answer. Do not say the item numbers.

SAY:
14. Be sure to move your marker so you can see all of the answer choices. Darken the circle for the number that tells *about how many centimeters long the chain is.*
15. Place your marker under the next row, the one with the four items. Look carefully at the items. Darken the circle for the item that is *shaped like a sphere...shaped like a sphere.*
16. Place your marker under the next row, the one with the leaves and the branch. Darken the circle for the number that tells *about how many leaves long the branch is.*
17. Place your marker under the next row, the one with the pictures of the clocks. Darken the circle for the clock that shows *three-thirty...three-thirty.*

Look at the arrow with the words *GO ON* at the bottom of the page. This tells you to go to the next page and continue working on the test.

SAY: **Now look at page 35.**

Check to see that all students find page 35.

SAY: **Now we will continue the test. Place your marker under the first row, the one with the calendar.**

Check to see that all students find item 18. Allow students time after each item to choose and mark their answer. Do not say the item numbers.

SAY:
18. Place your marker under the next row, the one with the calendar of November. Darken the circle for the date of *the fourth Thursday in November.*
19. Place your marker under the next row, the one with the diamond figure. Darken the circle for the number that tells *how many corners there are on this figure.*

20 Place your marker under the next row, the one with the pattern of shapes. Be sure to move your marker so you can see the answer choices. Darken the circle for *the two shapes that come next in this pattern*.

21 Place your marker under the last row on the page, the one that shows four items. Darken the circle for the item that is *shaped like a cone...shaped like a cone*.

SAY: **Look at the stop sign at the bottom of the page. You have completed the Unit 4 Test. Make sure that you have carefully filled in your answer spaces and have erased any stray marks. Then put your pencils down.**

After the test has been scored, review the questions and answer choices with students. If students are having difficulty, provide them with additional practice.

UNIT 5 Math Problems

Lesson 12: Working with Number Sentences

Mathematics Skills: Identifying and reading number sentences; using number sentences to solve problems; identifying number sentences that represent pictures

SAY: **Turn to Lesson 12, Working with Number Sentences, on page 36.**

Check to see that all students find Lesson 12. Introduce the Try This feature.

SAY: **In Lesson 12 you will practice choosing number sentences that match math problems you hear and see in pictures.**

Listen carefully. When I read a problem, you should try this: look at each picture. Think carefully about the information in the problem. Then find the number sentence that matches the problem you hear and see in the picture.

Place your marker under the first row, the one with the pictures of the bananas and the apples. Be sure to move your marker so you can see all the answer choices. This is the Sample. Now listen carefully. Darla went food shopping. First she put eight bananas into the basket. Then she put five apples into the basket. How many bananas and apples did Darla put into the basket altogether? Darla put eight bananas and five apples into the basket. Darken the circle next to the number sentence that shows *how to find the number of bananas and apples that Darla put into the basket*.

Allow students time to choose and mark their answer. Remind students to carefully fill in the answer space and to completely erase any stray marks. Then introduce the Think it Through feature.

SAY: **Now we will think it through. We will check the answer. You should have darkened the circle for the number sentence, 8 + 5 = ☐. This sentence reads *eight plus five equals blank*. The word *altogether* tells you that you must add. Darla had eight bananas and five apples. To find how many Darla had altogether, you would use the number sentence 8 + 5 = ☐.**

Check to see that all students have filled in the correct answer space. If students have not filled in the correct answer space, caution them to completely erase their incorrect answer and to erase any stray marks before they darken the correct space. Remind students that they were instructed to choose the number sentence that shows *how many bananas and apples Darla had altogether*.

Ask students if they have any questions about the Sample or about darkening the answer space.

SAY: **Now you will practice choosing more number sentences that match math problems you hear and see in pictures. Listen carefully to each problem. Then choose your answer from the number sentences given for the problem.**

Now we will begin. Place your marker under the next row. Make sure you move your marker so you can see all the answer choices. Look at the picture of the ducks.

Check to see that all students find item 1. Allow students time after each item to choose and mark their answer. Do not say the item numbers.

SAY: 1 **Theodore saw nine ducks in the pond in the park. Then four of the ducks swam away to the other side of the pond. How many ducks were left? Darken the circle for *the* number sentence that shows *how to find out how many ducks were left*.**

2 **Place your marker under the next row, the one with the picture of the frogs. Look at the picture of the frogs. Darken the circle for the number sentence that best shows *what is happening in the picture*.**

Look at the stop sign at the bottom of the page. You have now finished the lesson and should put your pencils down.

Review the questions and answer choices with students. Discuss with the class why one answer is correct and the others are not correct. Also check to see that students have carefully filled in their answer spaces and have completely erased any stray marks.

Lesson 13: Solving Problems

Mathematics Skills: Using problem-solving strategies to solve one-step and multiple-step word problems; classifying geometric figures

SAY: **Turn to Lesson 13, Solving Problems, on page 37.**

Check to see that all students find Lesson 13. Introduce the Try This feature.

SAY: **In Lesson 13 you will practice choosing pictures and numbers that answer math problems you hear.**

Listen carefully. When I read a problem, you should try this: look at each picture or number for the problem. Think carefully about the information in the problem. Then find the picture or number that answers the problem you hear.

Place your marker under the first row, the one with the pictures of the cans of tennis balls. Be sure to move your marker so you can see all the answer choices. This is the Sample. You will mark the answer next to the correct answer choice. Now listen carefully. Mr. Lu owns a sporting goods store. He had 10 cans of tennis balls. Then he sold 4 cans. How many cans of tennis balls did Mr. Lu have left? Darken the circle next to *the picture that best shows what happened in the story.*

Allow students time to choose and mark their answer. Remind students to carefully fill in the answer space and to completely erase any stray marks. Then introduce the Think it Through feature.

SAY: **Now we will think it through. We will check the answer. You should have darkened the circle next to the second picture. It shows 10 cans with an "X" over the last 4 cans. Since Mr. Lu had 10 cans and he sold 4 cans, you would subtract 4 from 10. This picture is the correct answer because it best shows what happened in the story.**

Check to see that all students have filled in the correct answer space. If students have not filled in the correct answer space, caution them to completely erase their incorrect answer and to erase any stray marks before they darken the correct space. Remind students that they were instructed to choose *the picture that best shows what happened in the story.*

Ask students if they have any questions about the Sample or about darkening the answer space.

SAY: **Now you will practice choosing more pictures and numbers that answer math problems you hear. Listen carefully to each problem. Then choose your answer from the pictures or numbers given for the problem.**

Now we will begin. Place your marker under the next row, the one with the numbers.

Check to see that all students find item 1. Allow students time after each item to choose and mark their answer. Do not say the item numbers.

SAY: 1 **Look at the numbers. Listen to this riddle about a number. I am thinking of a number that is more than twelve and less than twenty-five. It has a three in it. What number am I thinking of? It is more than twelve, less than twenty-five, and has a three in it. Darken the circle for the number *that I am thinking of.***

2 **Place your marker under the next row, the one with the shapes. Look at each shape carefully. Which one is different from the others? Darken the circle for *the shape that does not belong.***

3 **Place your marker under the last row on the page. Look at the coins in the picture. Listen to this story. Anita has the coins shown in the picture. Think about how much money the coins are worth. How much more will Anita need to have a total of thirty cents? Darken the circle for the number that shows *how much more Anita will need to have thirty cents.***

Look at the arrow with the words *GO ON* at the bottom of the page. This tells you to go to the next page and continue working on the lesson.

SAY: **Now turn to page 38.**

Check to see that all students find page 38.

SAY: **Now we will continue the lesson. Place your marker under the first row, the one with the pictures of the oranges.**

Check to see that all students find item 4. Allow students time after each item to choose and mark their answer. Do not say the item numbers.

SAY: 4 **Look at the pictures of the oranges. Listen to this story. Ray is packing oranges into a bag for a family hiking trip. He must put six more oranges into the bag to make twelve oranges in all. How many oranges does Ray have in the bag now? Ray must put six more oranges into the bag to make twelve. Darken the circle** for the picture that shows *how many oranges Ray has in the bag now*.

5 Place your marker under the last row on the page. Look at the pictures of the coins. Be sure to move your marker so you can see all of the answer choices. You will mark your answer next to the correct answer. Listen to this story. Erika has twenty-five cents. Sally has ten cents less than Erika. Kate has more money than Sally. How much money could Kate have? Darken the circle next to the picture that shows *how much money Kate could have*.

Look at the stop sign at the bottom of the page. You have now finished the lesson and should put your pencils down.

Review the questions and answer choices with students. Discuss with the class why one answer is correct and the others are not correct. Also check to see that students have carefully filled in their answer spaces and have completely erased any stray marks.

Lesson 14: Working with Statistics and Probability

Mathematics Skills: Reading and interpreting picture graphs; determining simple probability

SAY: **Turn to Lesson 14, Working with Statistics and Probability, on page 39.**

Check to see that all students find Lesson 14. Introduce the Try This feature.

SAY: **In Lesson 14 you will practice reading and answering questions about picture graphs and other math problems.**

Listen carefully. When I read a problem, you should try this: Think carefully about the information in the problem. Then find the picture or number that answers the problem you hear.

Place your marker under the first row, the one with the picture of the basket and the fruit. This is the Sample. Now listen carefully. Look at the fruit in the basket. Now look at the other fruit in the row. Which fruit could you choose from the basket? Darken the circle under *the picture of the fruit that you could choose from the basket*.

Allow students time to choose and mark their answer. Remind students to carefully fill in the answer space and to completely erase any stray marks. Then introduce the Think it Through feature.

SAY: **Now we will think it through. We will check the answer. In the basket there is an apple, a bunch of grapes, and a banana. You should have darkened the circle for the second answer choice. The bunch of grapes is the only fruit that you could choose from the basket. The other fruits—an orange, a cherry, and a peach—are not in the basket. The correct answer choice is the bunch of grapes.**

Check to see that all students have filled in the correct answer space. If students have not filled in the correct answer space, caution them to completely erase their incorrect answer and to erase any stray marks before they darken the correct space. Remind students that they were instructed to choose *the picture of the fruit that they could choose from the basket*.

Ask students if they have any questions about the Sample or about darkening the answer space.

SAY: **Now you will practice reading and answering more questions about picture graphs and other math problems. Listen carefully to each problem. Then choose your answer from the pictures or numbers given for the problem.**

Now we will begin. Look at the picture graph titled *Bear Sightings*. This graph shows how many bears Kim and her family saw while they were camping in a national park. Look at the sentence under the graph. This helps you to read the graph correctly. You will use this graph to answer questions 1 through 3. Now place your marker under the next row.

Check to see that all students find item 1. Allow students time after each item to choose and mark their answer. Do not say the item numbers.

SAY: 1 **Darken the circle for the number that tells *how many bears Kim and her family saw on Thursday, their first day at the park*.**

2 **Place your marker under the next row. Darken the circle for the number that tells *which day Kim and her family saw the fewest number of bears*.**

3 **Place your marker under the last row on the page. Darken the circle for the number that shows *how many more bears Kim and her family saw on Sunday than on Monday*.**

Look at the arrow with the words *GO ON* at the bottom of the page. This tells you to go to the next page and continue working on the lesson.

SAY: **Now turn to page 40.**

Check to see that all students find page 40.

SAY: **Now we will continue the lesson. Look at**

the picture graph titled *Musical Instruments Played by Students*. This graph shows what instruments students in the band play. You will use this graph to answer questions 4 through 6. Now place your marker under the first row. Listen carefully.

Check to see that all students find item 4. Allow students time after each item to choose and mark their answer. Do not say the item numbers.

4. Darken the circle for the instrument that *most students play*.
5. Place your marker under the next row. Darken the circle for the number that tells *how many students altogether play drum and piano*.
6. Place your marker under the next row. Darken the circle for the number that tells *how many more students play guitars than trumpets*.
7. Place your marker under the last row on the page. Look at the tray and the items on the tray. Now look at the other items in the row. Darken the circle for the item that *you could take off the tray*.

Look at the stop sign at the bottom of the page. You have finished the lesson and should put your pencils down.

Review the questions and answer choices with students. Discuss with the class why one answer is correct and the others are not correct. Also check to see that students have carefully filled in their answer spaces and have completely erased any stray marks.

UNIT 5 Test

SAY: **Turn to the Unit 5 Test on page 41.**

Check to see that all students find the Unit 5 Test.

SAY: **In this test you will choose pictures and numbers that answer math problems you hear and see. Place your marker under the first row, the one with the pictures of the ears of corn and the carrots. This is the <u>Sample</u>. Make sure to move your marker so you can see all of the answer choices.**

Now listen carefully. Ann Marie went to the vegetable market. There she bought some ears of corn and some carrots. She bought seven ears of corn and three carrots. How many vegetables did Ann Marie buy altogether? Darken the circle next to the number sentence that shows *how to find the number of vegetables that Ann Marie bought*.

Allow students time to choose and mark their answer. Remind students that they were instructed to find the number sentence that shows *how to find the number of vegetables that Ann Marie bought*.

SAY: **You should have darkened the circle next to the number sentence, $7 + 3 = \square$. This sentence reads *seven plus three equals blank*. The word *altogether* tells you that you must add. Ann Marie bought seven ears of corn and three carrots. To find how many Ann Marie bought altogether, you would use the number sentence $7 + 3 = \square$.**

Check to see that all students have filled in the correct answer space. Ask students if they have any questions.

SAY: **Now you will choose more pictures and numbers that answer math problems. Listen carefully to each problem. Then choose your answer from the pictures or numbers given in the row. Place your marker under the next row, the one with the picture of the chicks.**

Check to see that all students find item 1. Allow students time after each item to choose and mark their answer. Do not say the item numbers.

SAY: 1. **Listen to this story. Felipe went to visit his grandmother on her farm. He went to the hen house to see some new baby chicks. One hen had ten baby chicks. Another hen had four baby chicks. How many baby chicks did Felipe see altogether? One hen had ten baby chicks. Another hen had four baby chicks. Darken the circle next to the number sentence that shows *how to find the number of baby chicks that Felipe saw*.**
2. **Place your marker under the next row, the one with the picture of the kittens. Make sure you move your marker so you can see all the answer choices. Darken the circle for the number sentence that shows *what is happening in the picture*.**
3. **Place your marker under the next row, the one with the shapes. Look at each shape carefully. Which one is different from the others? Darken the circle for *the shape that does not belong*.**

Look at the arrow with the words *GO ON* at the bottom of the page. This tells you to go to the next page and continue working on the test.

SAY: **Now turn to page 42.**

Check to see that all students find page 42.

SAY: **Now we will continue the test. Place your**

marker under the first row.

Check to see that all students find item 4. Allow students time after each item to choose and mark their answer. Do not say the item numbers.

SAY: 4 Lee's mother bought nine cookies at a bakery. Lee and his two sisters ate three of the cookies. Darken the circle beside the number sentence that best shows *what is happening in the picture.*

5 Place your marker under the next row, the one with the numbers. Listen to this riddle about a number. I am thinking of a number that is less than thirty-eight. You say its name when you count by fives. It has a two in it. What number am I thinking of? It is less than thirty-eight, you say it when you count by fives, and it has a two in it. Darken the circle for *the number that I am thinking of.*

6 Place your marker under the next row, the one with the pictures of the party hats. Listen to this story. Kareem is having a birthday party. He invited nine friends to the party. He needs to get four more hats. How many party hats does he have already? Kareem invited nine friends and needs four more hats. Darken the circle for the picture that shows *how many hats Kareem has already.*

7 Place your marker under the next row. Look at the pictures of the coins. Listen to this story. Nelson has the coins shown in the picture. Think about how much money the coins are worth. How much more will Nelson need to have a total of fifty cents? Darken the circle for the number that shows *how much more Nelson will need to have fifty cents.*

Look at the arrow with the words GO ON at the bottom of the page. This tells you to go to the next page and continue working on the test.

SAY: **Now look at page 43.**

Check to see that all students find page 43.

SAY: **Now we will continue the test. Place your marker under the first row, the one that has the pictures of flowers.**

Check to see that all students find item 8. Allow students time after each item to choose and mark their answer. Do not say the item numbers.

SAY: 8 Listen to this story. Cheng went to the town art fair today. He saw some beautiful handmade silk flowers. He decided to buy a couple of them for his grandmother. He had twenty-five cents to spend. Now look at the flowers and their price tags. Darken the circle for *the two flowers Cheng could buy with exactly twenty-five cents.*

SAY: **Look at the picture graph titled *Pet Store*. This graph shows a number of pets for sale in a local store. You will use this graph to answer questions 9 through 11. Now place your marker under the next row.**

Check to see that all students find item 9. Allow students time after each item to choose and mark their answer. Do not say the item numbers.

SAY: 9 Darken the circle for the number that tells *how many mice there are in the pet store.*

10 Place your marker under the next row. Trina bought three fish at the pet store. Darken the circle for the number that shows *how many fish were then left at the store.*

11 Place your marker under the next row. How many more rabbits than birds does the pet store have? Darken the circle for the number that tells *how many more rabbits than birds there are in the pet store.*

SAY: **Look at the stop sign at the bottom of the page. You have completed the Unit 5 Test. Make sure that you have carefully filled in your answer spaces and have erased any stray marks. Then put your pencils down.**

After the test has been scored, review the questions and answer choices with students. If students are having difficulty, provide them with additional practice.

UNIT 6 Math Procedures

Lesson 15: Using Computation in Word Problems

Mathematics Skills: Applying addition and subtraction to word problems

SAY: **Turn to Lesson 15, Using Computation in Word Problems, on page 44.**

Check to see that all students find Lesson 15. Introduce the Try This feature.

SAY: **In Lesson 15 you will practice adding and subtracting numbers to answer word problems you hear.**

Listen carefully. When I read a problem, you should try this: think carefully about the information in the problem. Then find the number that answers the problem you hear.

Place your marker under the first row, the one with the pictures of the turtles. This is the Sample. Now listen carefully. Selena had four turtles. She got two more for her birthday. How many turtles did she have altogether? Selena had four turtles and got two more. Darken the circle for the number that tells *how many turtles she had altogether.*

Allow students time to choose and mark their answer. Remind students to carefully fill in the answer space and to completely erase any stray marks. Then introduce the Think it Through feature.

SAY: **Now we will think it through. We will check the answer. You should have darkened the circle for the number** *6. Four turtles plus two turtles equals six turtles altogether.* **The correct answer is** *6.*

Check to see that all students have filled in the correct answer space. If students have not filled in the correct answer space, caution them to completely erase their incorrect answer and to erase any stray marks before they darken the correct space. Remind students that they were instructed to choose a number that tells *how many turtles Selena had altogether.*

Ask students if they have any questions about the Sample or about darkening the answer space.

SAY: **Now you will practice adding and subtracting more numbers that answer word problems you hear. Listen carefully to each problem. Then choose your answer from the numbers given for the problem.**

Now we will begin. Place your marker under the next row. Look at the pictures of the orange and the pineapple.

Check to see that all students find item 1. Allow students time after each item to choose and mark their answer. Do not say the item numbers.

SAY: 1 **Listen carefully to this story. Ira put nine oranges in a bag. He also put two pineapples in the bag. How many more oranges than pineapples are in the bag? There are nine oranges and two pineapples in the bag. Darken the circle for the number that tells** *how many more oranges than pineapples are in the bag.*

2 **Place your marker under the next row, the one with the pictures of the calculators. Mrs. Ling had fifteen calculators in her store. She sold seven of the calculators. How many calculators did she have left? There were fifteen calculators and seven were sold. Darken the circle for the number that tells** *how many calculators were left.*

3 **Place your marker under the next row, the one with the pictures of fish. Renee and Joel went fishing. Renee caught fourteen fish. Joel caught fifteen fish. How many fish did they catch altogether? Renee caught fourteen fish and Joel caught fifteen fish. Darken the circle for the number that tells** *how many fish they caught altogether.*

4 **Place your marker under the next row, the one with the numbers. Mrs. Tanaka had seventy-five cents. She gave her son fifty cents. How much money did she have left? Mrs. Tanaka had seventy-five cents and gave fifty cents to her son. Darken the circle for** *the amount of money she had left.*

5 **Place your marker under the last row on the page. Look at the bottles of juice. There were six bottles of juice in the box. Meili gave five bottles of juice to her friends. Darken the circle for the number that tells** *how many juice bottles are left.*

Look at the stop sign at the bottom of the page. You have now finished the lesson and should put your pencils down.

Review the questions and answer choices with students. Discuss with the class why one answer is correct and the others are not correct. Also check to see that students have carefully filled in their answer spaces and have completely erased any stray marks.

Lesson 16: Using Computation

Mathematics Skills: Adding and subtracting whole numbers with and without regrouping

SAY: **Turn to Lesson 16, Using Computation, on page 45.**

Check to see that all students find Lesson 16. Introduce the Try This feature.

SAY: **In Lesson 16 you will practice adding or subtracting numbers to find the answers to math problems you read.**

Listen carefully. When you read a problem, you should try this: **add or subtract the numbers in your head. Then find the number that answers the problem.**

Place your marker under the first row. This is the Sample. Listen carefully. Darken the circle for the number that is *closest in value to thirty-five plus twenty-three.*

Allow students time to choose and mark their answer. Remind students to carefully fill in the answer space and to completely erase any stray marks. Then introduce the Think it Through feature.

SAY: **Now we will think it through. We will check the answer. You should have darkened the circle for the last number, *60*. If you add 35 and 23, the answer is 58. *Fifty-eight* is closest in value to the number *sixty*. The correct answer is *60*.**

Check to see that all students have filled in the correct answer space. If students have not filled in the correct answer space, caution them to completely erase their incorrect answer and to erase any stray marks before they darken the correct space. Remind students that they were instructed to find the number closest in value to *thirty-five plus twenty-three*.

Ask students if they have any questions about the Sample or about darkening the answer space.

SAY: **Now you will practice adding or subtracting more numbers. Do numbers 1 through 5 on your own. Listen carefully. Read each problem. Then find the correct answer given among the answer choices. The last answer in each problem is *NG*. *NG* stands for *Not Given*. This means that the answer does not appear as one of the answer choices. If you add or subtract the problems and find that the answer is not among the answer choices, darken the circle for *NG*. When you come to the stop sign at the bottom of the page, put your pencils down.**

Place your marker under the next row. You may now begin.

Allow students time to choose and mark their answers.

Review the questions and answer choices with students. Discuss with the class why one answer is correct and the others are not correct. Also check to see that students have carefully filled in their answer spaces and have completely erased any stray marks.

UNIT 6 Test

SAY: **Turn to the Unit 6 Test on page 46.**

Check to see that all students find the Unit 6 Test.

SAY: **In this test you will add or subtract numbers that answer math problems you hear or read. Place your marker under the first row, the one with the picture of the goldfish. This is Sample A. Now listen carefully. Anton had eight goldfish. He bought three more. How many goldfish did he have then? Anton had eight goldfish and bought three more. Darken the circle for the number that tells *how many goldfish Anton had altogether*.**

Allow students time to choose and mark their answer. Remind students that they were instructed to find the number that tells how many goldfish Anton had altogether.

SAY: **You should have darkened the circle for the third number, *11*. *Eight goldfish plus three goldfish equals eleven goldfish*. The correct answer is *11*.**

Ask students if they have any questions.

SAY: **Now place your marker under the next row. This is Sample B. Look at the number sentence at the beginning of the row. The problem reads *forty-three minus thirty-one*. Look at the answer choices. The last answer choice is *NG*. *NG* means *Not Given*. If you add or subtract a problem in this test and the answer is not among the answer choices, darken the circle for *NG*.**

Ask students if they have any questions.

SAY: **Now work Sample B on your own.**

Allow students time to choose and mark their answer. Remind students that they were instructed to find the number that answers the problem *forty-three minus thirty-one*.

SAY: **You should have darkened the circle for *NG*. *If you subtract 31 from 43, the answer is 12.* Twelve is not given as an answer choice, so *NG* is the correct answer.**

Check to see that all students have filled in the correct answer spaces.

Ask students if they have any questions.

SAY: **Now you will add or subtract more numbers to find the answers to math problems you hear or read. Choose your answer from the numbers given in the row. Place your marker under the next row, the one with the fireflies.**

Make sure all students find item 1. Allow students time after each item to choose and mark their answer. Do not say the item numbers.

SAY: 1 **Mel saw nine fireflies on one bush. Then he saw four fireflies on another bush. How many fireflies did Mel see altogether? There were nine fireflies and four fireflies. Darken the circle for the number that tells *how many fireflies Mel saw altogether*.**

2 **Place your marker under the next row. Look at the raccoons. Gabby saw this number of raccoons near the camp site the first night that she and her family were on vacation. She saw three more**

raccoons the next night. Darken the circle for *the number of raccoons Gabby saw altogether on vacation*.

3   Place your marker under the next row, the one with the giraffes. Anthony and Kathy went to Brookfield Zoo with their class. Anthony saw ten giraffes in the morning. Kathy saw six giraffes in the afternoon. How many more giraffes did Anthony see than Kathy? Anthony saw ten giraffes and Kathy saw six. Darken the circle for the number that tells *how many more giraffes Anthony saw than Kathy*.

4   Place your marker under the next row, the one with the bees. Mr. Chin saw this number of bees in a field of clover. Seven flew away. Darken the circle for the number that tells *how many bees are left*.

Look at the arrow with the words GO ON at the bottom of the page. This tells you to go to the next page and continue working on the test.

SAY: **Now look at page 47.**

Check to see that all students find page 47.

SAY: **Now we will continue the test. Place your marker under the first row.**

Check to see that all students find item 5.

SAY: 5   **Look at the amount of money. Dan had fifty cents. He bought a toy car for thirty cents. How much money did he have left? Dan had fifty cents and bought a toy car for thirty cents. Darken the circle for *the amount of money he had left*.**

6   **Place your marker under the next row. Now listen carefully. Darken the circle for the number that is *closest in value to forty-nine minus twenty-three*.**

Allow students time to choose and mark their answer.

SAY: **Listen carefully. Now you will practice adding or subtracting more numbers that answer math problems you read. You will do problems 7 through 11 on your own. Read each problem. Find the correct answer given among the answer choices. If you cannot find the correct answer, darken the circle for NG. When you come to the stop sign at the bottom of the page, put your pencils down. You may now begin.**

Allow students time to choose and mark their answers.

SAY: **It is now time to stop. You have completed the Unit 6 Test. Make sure that you have carefully filled in your answer spaces and have completely erased any stray marks. Then put your pencils down and close your books.**

After the test has been scored, review the questions and answer choices with students. If students are having difficulty, provide them with additional practice.

UNIT 7 Language

Lesson 17: Building Listening Skills

Language Skills: Listening to remember stated details, sequences, and directions; drawing conclusions; making inferences; matching pictures that rhyme with words to complete poems; distinguishing between reality and fantasy

SAY: **Turn to Lesson 17, Building Listening Skills, on page 48.**

Check to see that all students find Lesson 17. Introduce the Try This feature.

SAY: **In Lesson 17 you will practice choosing pictures that answer questions about stories you hear.**

Listen carefully. When I read a story, you should try this: listen very carefully. Look at the pictures for the story. Then find the picture that answers the question about the story.

Place your marker under the first row. This is the Sample. Now listen carefully. It was Saturday and it was raining. Mei could not go out to play with her friends. After she ate lunch, Mei told her mother, "I have nothing to do. What can I do that's fun?" Her mother asked, "Why don't you watch TV?" But Mei said she didn't want to watch TV. Then Mei's mother showed her a trunk filled with old clothes, purses, hats, and other things. Mei's mother said, "Here, use your imagination and have fun." Darken the circle for the picture *that shows how Mei had fun on a rainy Saturday*.

Allow students time to choose and mark their answer. Remind students to carefully fill in the answer space and to completely erase any stray marks. Then introduce the Think it Through feature.

SAY: **Now we will think it through. We will check the answer. You should have darkened the circle for the *third picture*. Mei dressed in some of the clothes and things she found in the trunk. She had fun playing dress-up and using her imagination.**

Check to see that all students have filled in the correct answer space. If students have not filled in the correct answer space, caution them to completely erase their incorrect answer and to erase any stray marks before they darken the correct space. Remind students that they were instructed to choose the picture that showed *how Mei had fun on a rainy Saturday*.

Ask students if they have any questions about the Sample or about darkening the answer space.

SAY: **Now you will practice choosing more pictures that answer questions about stories you hear. Listen carefully to each story. Then choose your answer from the pictures given for the story.**

Now we will begin. Place your marker under the next row. Look at the pictures of the man. Listen to this story.

Check to see that all students find item 1. Allow students time after each item to choose and mark their answer. Do not say the item numbers.

SAY: 1 **Mr. Henson was building a new doghouse for his dog, Grover. First, he sawed the wood into the pieces that he needed. Next, he nailed the pieces together to make the doghouse. Finally, he painted Grover's new doghouse. Darken the circle for the picture that shows *what Mr. Henson did first*.**

2 **Place your marker under the next row. Look at the pictures of the animals. Frankie's father gave him a box with a new pet in it. When Frankie looked into the box, he saw long ears and a short, fluffy tail. Darken the circle for the picture that shows *Frankie's new pet*.**

3 **Place your marker under the next row. Listen to this poem.**

*My Grandmother lives in the state of Maine
When we go to visit her, we travel by
_____.*

Darken the circle for the picture that will *rhyme with the poem*.

4 **Place your marker under the last row on the page. Look at the pictures of the plate and the spoons and forks. Elena and Ricardo were helping their mother by setting the table for dinner. Elena placed the spoon and fork on either side of the plate. Ricardo crossed the spoon and fork and put them on the plate. Then the spoon cried, "That's not right!," and it jumped off the plate. Darken the circle for the picture that shows *something that could not happen*.**

Look at the stop sign at the bottom of the page. You have now finished the lesson and should put your pencils down.

Review the questions and answer choices with students. Discuss with the class why one answer is correct and the others are not correct. Also check to see that students have carefully filled in their answer spaces and have completely erased any stray marks.

Lesson 18: Prewriting, Composing, and Editing

Language Skills: Determining the purpose for writing; determining appropriate topics; organizing information and ideas; determining topic relevance; alphabetizing words; using the parts of a book to locate information; determining correct sentence order; identifying extraneous information in paragraphs; identifying correctly applied grammar; identifying correct capitalization and punctuation; identifying correctly and effectively written sentences

SAY: **Turn to Lesson 18, Prewriting, Composing, and Editing, on page 49.**

Check to see that all students find Lesson 18. Introduce the Try This feature.

SAY: **In Lesson 18 you will practice finding words and sentences that answer questions about stories you hear.**

Listen carefully. When I read a story, you should try this: listen very carefully. Look at the answer choices for the story. Then find the one that best answers the question.

Place your marker under the first row. Be sure to move your marker so you can see all the answer choices. This is Sample A.

Check to see that all students find Sample A.

SAY: **Look at the picture under the title *Julia's Ocean Trip* while I read you a story about Julia. Now listen carefully. Julia's family is taking a boat trip to Mexico. She is keeping a journal about all the things she does in Mexico. Which activity will not be in Julia's journal? Is it *Games we play on the ship*, *Shopping in the market*, or *Swimming in the ocean*? Darken the circle beside the activity *which will not be in Julia's journal*.**

Allow students time to choose and mark their answer. Remind students to carefully fill in the answer space and to completely erase any stray marks. Then introduce the Think it Through feature.

SAY: **Now we will think it through. We will check**

the answer. You should have darkened the circle for the first answer, *Games we play on the ship*. This is the correct answer. This activity does not belong in Julia's journal because Julia is keeping a journal about things she does in Mexico. This activity takes place on the ship, not in Mexico.

Check to see that all students have filled in the correct answer space. If students have not filled in the correct answer space, caution them to completely erase their incorrect answer and to erase any stray marks before they darken the correct space. Remind students that they were instructed to choose *which activity Julia will not write about in her journal*.

SAY: **Place your marker under the next row. This is Sample B.**

Check to see that all students find Sample B.

SAY: **This is what Julia wrote on one page of her journal. Read it silently to yourself as I read it aloud.**

*We swam in the water.
And played in the waves.
We made sand castles.*

Which group of words is not a complete sentence? Is it *We swam in the water*, *And played in the waves*, or *We made sand castles*? Darken the circle beside the words that *do not make a complete sentence*.

Allow students time to choose and mark their answer. Then introduce the Think it Through feature.

SAY: **Now we will think it through. We will check the answer. You should have darkened the circle for the second answer. The correct answer is *And played in the waves*. These words do not make a complete sentence.**

Check to see that all students have filled in the correct answer space. Remind students that they were instructed to choose the words that did not make a complete sentence.

SAY: **Place your marker under the next row. This is Sample C.**

Check to see that all students find Sample C.

SAY: **This is what Julia wrote on another page of her journal. Read it silently to yourself as I read it aloud.**

*Shopping was fun.
Mother buyed me a hat.*

Look at the underlined word. Did Julia use the right word? Should she write *bought*, *buy*, or is the underlined word *Correct the way it is*? Darken the circle for *the way Julia should write the underlined word*.

Allow students time to choose and mark their answer. Then introduce the Think it Through feature.

SAY: **Now we will think it through. We will check the answer. You should have darkened the circle for the first answer. The correct answer is *bought*. Julia should write *Mother bought me a hat*.**

Check to see that all students have filled in the correct answer space. Remind students that they were instructed to choose *the way Julia should write the underlined word*.

Ask students if they have any questions about the Samples or about darkening the answer space.

SAY: **Look at the arrow with the words *GO ON* at the bottom of the page. This tells you to go to the next page and continue working on the lesson.**

SAY: **Now turn to page 50.**

Check to see that all students find page 50.

SAY: **Now you will practice finding more words and sentences that answer questions about stories you hear. Listen carefully to each story. Then choose your answer from the words and sentences given. Place your marker under the first row. Be sure to move your marker so you can see all the answer choices. Look at the picture under the title *Lenny's Horse* while I read you a story about Lenny. Then you will answer some questions about this story. Now listen carefully.**

Check to see that all students find item 1. Allow students time after each item to choose and mark their answer.

SAY: 1 **Lenny's teacher asked the class to write a story about their pets. Lenny has a horse. He decided to write about the tricks his horse can do. Why is Lenny writing a story? Is it *to tell why he loves horses*, *to tell how to teach a horse tricks*, or *to tell a story about his pet*? Darken the circle for the answer that tells *why Lenny is writing a story*.**

2 **Place your marker under the next row. Lenny used these words in his story: *tricks*, *kiss*, and *hand*. He wanted to look them up in the dictionary to make sure they were spelled correctly. Darken the circle for**

the word that would be *listed first in alphabetical (ABC) order in the dictionary.*

SAY: **Look at the first part of Lenny's story, under the title** *Fun with My Horse.* **Read it silently to yourself as I read it aloud.**

Check to see that all students find *Fun with My Horse.*

SAY: *Fun with My Horse*

My horse can do many tricks.
He lifts his leg to my hand shake.
He gives me a kiss with his nose.
My horse can also play hiding games.

SAY: **Now you will answer some questions. Place your marker under the next row. Be sure to move your marker so you can see all the answer choices.**

Check to see that all students find item 3. Allow students time after each item to choose and mark their answer.

SAY: 3 **Look at the underlined sentence that reads** *He lifts his leg to my hand shake.* **Did Lenny write the sentence correctly? Should he write** *He lifts his leg to hand shake my, He lifts his leg to shake my hand,* **or is the sentence** *Correct the way it is*? **Darken the circle for** *the way Lenny should write the sentence.*

4 **Place your marker under the last row on the page. Lenny wanted to describe his horse. Would he write** *My horse is brown and white, I like to see my horse run,* **or** *My horse comes when he sees me*? **Darken the circle for** *the sentence Lenny will write to describe his horse.*

Look at the arrow with the words *GO ON* **at the bottom of the page. This tells you to go to the next page and continue working on the lesson.**

SAY: **Now go to page 51.**

Check to see that all students find page 51.

SAY: **Now we will continue the lesson. Look at the rest of Lenny's story at the top of the page. Listen to what Lenny wrote next in his story. Read it silently to yourself as I read it aloud.**

Check to see that all students find the sentence with the number *1* below it.

SAY: *I gived my horse a treat after each trick.*
　　(1)
He likes carrots best.
　　(2)

If I forget his treat, he shakes his head.

SAY: **Now place your marker under the first row.**

Check to see that all students find item 5. Allow students time after each item to choose and mark their answer.

SAY: 5 **Look at the underlined word,** *gived,* **with the number** *1* **under it. Did Lenny use the right word? Should he write** *gave, give,* **or is the word** *Correct the way it is*? **Darken the circle for the way Lenny should write** *the underlined word.*

6 **Place your marker under the next row. Look at the underlined word,** *likes,* **with the number** *2* **under it. Did Lenny use the right word? Should he write** *like, liked,* **or is the word** *Correct the way it is*? **Darken the circle for the way Lenny should** *write the underlined word.*

Ask students if they have any questions.

SAY: **Now I will read you another story. Look at the picture under the title** *How People Travel.*

Check to see that all students find *How People Travel.*

SAY: **Now listen while I read you a story about Keisha. Keisha is writing a report about how people travel from place to place. She put a Table of Contents at the front of her report. Read it silently to yourself as I read it aloud. Chapter 1 is called** *On Tracks* **and begins on page 6. Chapter 2 is called** *In Air* **and begins on page 21. Chapter 3 is called** *Over Land* **and begins on page 38. Chapter 4 is called** *By Water* **and begins on page 50. Now place your marker under the next row.**

Check to see that all students find item 7. Allow students time after each item to choose and mark their answer.

SAY: 7 **Look at the Table of Contents again. Would Keisha write about ships on page** *21,* **page** *38,* **or page** *50*? **Darken the circle for** *the page on which Keisha would write about ships.*

8 **Place your marker under the last row on the page. Look at the Table of Contents. Would Keisha write about airplanes in chapter** *1, 2,* **or** *3*? **Darken the circle for the chapter in which Keisha would** *write about airplanes.*

Look at the arrow with the words *GO ON* **at the bottom of the page. This tells you to go to the next page and continue working on the lesson.**

SAY: **Now turn to page 52.**

Check to see that all students find page 52.

SAY: Now we will continue the lesson. Look at the title *Travel in the City*.

Check to see that all students find the title *Travel in the City*.

SAY: Listen to what Keisha wrote in her report. Read it silently to yourself as I read it aloud.

Travel in the City

*Many people drive cars.
In large cities.
Some people ride in taxis.
Most people ride the bus.*

SAY: Now place your marker under the first row.

Check to see that all students find item 9. Allow students time after each item to choose and mark their answer.

SAY: 9 Which sentence will Keisha write next? Will she write *A few people might walk to work*, *People work in a city*, or *The city is noisy*? Darken the circle for *the sentence Keisha will write next*.

10 Place your marker under the next row. Which sentence is not a complete sentence? Is it *Many people drive cars*, *In large cities*, or *Some people ride in taxis*? Darken the circle for the group of words that is *not a complete sentence*.

Ask students if they have any questions.

SAY: Now listen to what Keisha wrote next in her report. Read it silently to yourself as I read it aloud.

Check to see that all students find the sentence with the number *1* below it.

SAY: *We lives in the city.*
(1)
My father rides a bus to work.
(2)
It is too far for him to walk.

SAY: Now place your marker under the next row.

Check to see that all students find item 11. Allow students time after each item to choose and mark their answer.

SAY: 11 Look at the underlined words with the number *1* under them. Did Keisha use the right words? Should she write *We is living*, *We live*, or is the group of underlined words *Correct the way it is*? Darken the circle for *the way Keisha should write the underlined words*.

12 Place your marker under the last row on the page. Look at the underlined words with the number *2* under them. Did Keisha use the right words? Should she write *My Father*, *my father*, or is the group of words *Correct the way it is*? Darken the circle for *the way Keisha should write the group of underlined words*.

Look at the arrow with the words *GO ON* at the bottom of the page. This tells you to go to the next page and continue working on the lesson.

SAY: Now go to page 53.

Check to see that all students find page 53.

SAY: Now we will continue the lesson. Now I will read you another story. Look at the picture under the title *Father's Birthday Surprise* while I read you a story about Rita.

Check to see that all students find *Father's Birthday Surprise*.

SAY: Rita is planning a birthday surprise for her father. She wants to write a poem for her father. She wants to write about all the special things they do together. Now place your marker under the first row.

Check to see that all students find item 13. Allow students time after each item to choose and mark their answer.

SAY: 13 What should Rita do before writing her poem? Should she *bake her father a cake*, *make a list of the things they do together*, or *read a poem book*? Darken the circle that tells *what Rita should do first*.

14 Place your marker under the next row. What is this story about? Is it about *a birthday party*, *a present Rita will give her father*, or *things Rita and her father like to do*. Darken the circle that tells *what the story is about*.

Ask students if they have any questions.

SAY: Listen to the poem Rita wrote. It is called *Together*. Read it silently to yourself as I read it aloud.

Check to see that all students find the poem, *Together*.

SAY: *Together*

*Together we have fun.
We laugh and we run.
We fish in the lake.
And Mother likes to bake.
Sometimes we go on hikes.*

© Steck-Vaughn Publishing Company

Primary 1 Intro, SV 7165-1 **T31**

SAY: **Now place your marker under the next row.**

Check to see that all students find item 15. Allow students time after each item to choose and mark their answer.

SAY: 15 **Which sentence will Rita probably write next? Will she write** *And then we ride our bikes, I am happy,* **or** *You are fun*? **Darken the circle for the sentence** *that Rita will probably write next.*

16 **Now place your marker under the last row on the page. Which sentence does not belong in the poem? Is it** *Together we have fun, We fish in the lake,* **or** *And Mother likes to bake*? **Darken the circle for the sentence** *that does not belong in the poem.*

Look at the arrow with the words *GO ON* **at the bottom of the page. This tells you to go to the next page and continue working on the lesson.**

SAY: **Now turn to page 54.**

Check to see that all students find page 54.

SAY: **Now we will continue the lesson. Listen to the rest of the story about Rita. When Rita finished the poem, she wrote a letter at the bottom of her poem. Read the letter silently to yourself as I read it aloud.**

Check to see that all students find Rita's letter.

SAY: *Dear Father,*
(1)
Are you having a fun birthday
(2)
I wanted to make it special.
(3)
I love you.

Your daughter,
Rita

SAY: **Now place your marker under the next row.**

Check to see that all students find item 17. Allow students time after each item to choose and mark their answer.

SAY: 17 **Look at the underlined words with the number** *1* **under them. How should Rita write these words? Should she write** *Dear father, dear Father,* **or is the group of words** *Correct the way it is*? **Darken the circle for** *the way Rita should write the underlined words.*

18 **Place your marker under the next row. Look at the underlined word with the number** *2* **under it. Which punctuation mark should Rita write at the end of this sentence? Should she write a question mark, a period, or an exclamation point? Darken the circle for** *the punctuation mark Rita should write after the underlined word.*

19 **Place your marker under the last row on the page. Look at the words with the number** *3* **under them. How should Rita write these words? Should she write** *I wants, I wanting,* **or is the group of words** *Correct the way it is*? **Darken the circle for** *the way Rita should write the underlined words.*

SAY: **Look at the stop sign at the bottom of the page. You have now finished the lesson and should put your pencils down.**

Review the questions and answer choices with students. Discuss with the class why one answer is correct and the others are not correct. Also check to see that students have carefully filled in their answer spaces and have completely erased any stray marks.

Lesson 19: Finding Misspelled Words

Language Skills: Identifying misspelled words in the context of dictated sentences; recognizing the misspellings of sight words

SAY: **Turn to Lesson 19, Finding Misspelled Words, on page 55.**

Check to see that all students find Lesson 19. Introduce the Try This feature.

SAY: **In Lesson 19 you will practice finding words that are not spelled correctly.**

Listen carefully. I will read a sentence. Three of the words will be listed in the row. When I read a sentence, you should try this: look at each word. Then find the word that is not spelled correctly.

Place your marker under the first row. This is the Sample. Now listen carefully to this sentence. *I wint (went) along for the ride.* **Darken the circle next to the word that is** *not spelled correctly.*

Allow students time to choose and mark their answer. Remind students to carefully fill in the answer space and to completely erase any stray marks. Then introduce the Think it Through feature.

SAY: **Now we will think it through. We will check the answer. You should have darkened the circle for the first word.** *Went* **is the word that is not spelled correctly.** *Went* **should have an** *e* **where the** *i* **is.**

Check to see that all students have filled in the correct answer space. If students have not filled in the correct answer space, caution them to completely erase their incorrect answer and to erase any stray marks before they darken the correct space. Remind students that they were instructed to choose a word *that is not spelled correctly*.

Ask students if they have any questions about the Sample or about darkening the answer space.

SAY: **Now you will practice choosing more words that are not spelled correctly. Look at the words silently as I read the sentence aloud. Darken the circle for the word that is not spelled correctly. Now place your marker under the next row.**

Check to see that all students find item 1. Allow students time after each item to choose and mark their answer.

SAY: 1 **Listen to this sentence.** *Brian pickd (picked) these flowers.* **Darken the circle next to the word that is *not spelled correctly*.**
2 **Place your marker under the next row.** *It is Raúl's turn to wash dishs (dishes).* **Darken the circle next to the word that is *not spelled correctly*.**
3 **Place your marker under the next row.** *I can cros (cross) the street now.* **Darken the circle next to the word that is *not spelled correctly*.**
4 **Place your marker under the next row.** *Pleaze (please) pass the milk.* **Darken the circle next to the word that is *not spelled correctly*.**
5 **Place your marker under the next row.** *The frog sat on the gren (green) grass.* **Darken the circle next to the word that is *not spelled correctly*.**

SAY: **Now look at the top of the page. Find the next column. Place your marker under the first row.**

Check to see that all students find item 6. Allow students time after each item to choose and mark their answer.

SAY: 6 **Listen to this sentence.** *The two babies playd (played) quietly.* **Darken the circle next to the word that is *not spelled correctly*.**
7 **Place your marker under the next row.** *Tony walkt (walked) to the store by himself.* **Darken the circle next to the word that is *not spelled correctly*.**
8 **Place your marker under the next row.** *Those boyes (boys) joined the baseball team.* **Darken the circle next to the word that is *not spelled correctly*.**
9 **Place your marker under the next row.** *Alberto had a party at skool (school) today.* **Darken the circle next to the word that is *not spelled correctly*.**
10 **Place your marker under the next row.** *He wus (was) eating an apple.* **Darken the circle next to the word that is *not spelled correctly*.**
11 **Place your marker under the next row.** *Did you see the cake I bakt (baked)?* **Darken the circle next to the word that is *not spelled correctly*.**

SAY: **Look at the stop sign at the bottom of the page. You have now finished the lesson and should put your pencils down.**

Review the questions and answer choices with students. Discuss with the class why one answer is correct and the others are not correct. Also check to see that students have carefully filled in their answer spaces and have completely erased any stray marks.

UNIT 7 Test

SAY: **Turn to the Unit 7 Test on page 56.**

Check to see that all students find the Unit 7 Test.

SAY: **In the first part of the test you will choose pictures that answer questions about stories you hear. Place your marker under the first row. This is Sample A. Now listen carefully. Everyone said that the old house on Roland Road was haunted. No one had lived there for more than ten years. The house and yard were no longer cared for. Darken the circle for the picture that shows *how the house probably looked*.**

Allow students time to choose and mark their answer.

SAY: **You should have darkened the circle for the *second* picture. The second picture shows a house that needs to be fixed and trees that need to be trimmed.**

Check to see that all students have filled in the correct answer space. Ask students if they have any questions.

SAY: **Now you will choose more pictures that answer questions about stories you hear. Listen carefully to each story. Then choose your answer from the pictures given in the row. Place your marker under the next row.**

Check to see that all students find item 1. Allow students time after each item to choose and mark their answer.

© Steck-Vaughn Publishing Company

SAY: 1 Listen to this poem.

While we were walking by the lake
We saw a black and yellow _____.

Darken the circle for the picture that will *rhyme with the poem*.

2 Place your marker under the next row. Gloria was very busy on Saturday. She made her bed and then washed the dishes. When she was done, she went to her room to work on some homework. Darken the circle for the picture that shows *what Gloria did first*.

3 Place your marker under the next row. Inez and Isabel are twins. Even though they look alike, they are very different. They like to do different things. They wear their hair the same way, but they always dress differently. Darken the circle for the picture that shows *Inez and Isabel*.

4 Place your marker under the last row on the page. Chris and his family went to the lake. They saw a family of bears swimming across the lake. Then the bears joined Chris and his family at the picnic table for lunch. Later, Chris offered to clean up the mess at the picnic table. Darken the circle for the picture that shows *something that could not happen*.

Look at the arrow with the words GO ON at the bottom of the page. This tells you to go to the next page and continue working on the test.

SAY: **Now go to page 57.**

Check to see that all students find page 57.

SAY: **In the next part of the test I will ask you questions about stories you hear. Listen carefully to the story and questions. Then choose your answer from the words and sentences given. Place your marker under the first row. Be sure to move your marker so you can see all the answer choices. This is Sample B.**

Check to see that all students find Sample B.

SAY: **Look at the picture under the title *A New Friend* while I read you a story about Takashi.**

Check to see that all students find *A New Friend*.

SAY: **Now listen carefully. Takashi is writing a letter to a *pen pal*. A pen pal is a person that lives far away and someone the letter writer does not know. They write letters to each other. Takashi is telling the pen pal about himself.**

Which description will not be in Takashi's letter? Is it *What Takashi looks like*, *Why Takashi wants a pen pal*, or *Games Takashi likes to play*? Darken the circle beside the description *that will not be in Takashi's letter*.

Allow students time to choose and mark their answer.

SAY: **You should have darkened the circle for the *second answer*. The second answer does not describe Takashi.**

Check to see that all students have filled in the correct answer space.

SAY: **Place your marker under the next row. This is Sample C.**

Check to see that all students find Sample C.

SAY: **Listen carefully to the beginning of Takashi's letter. Read it silently to yourself as I read it aloud.**

Dear Paul,
I want to tell you about me.
I am in the first grade.
I like to play baseball.
Every day after school.

Which group of words is not a complete sentence? Is it *I am in the first grade*, *I like to play baseball*, or *Every day after school*? Darken the circle beside the words that *do not make a complete sentence*.

Allow students time to choose and mark their answer.

SAY: **You should have darkened the circle for the *last group of words*. These words do not make a complete sentence.**

Check to see that all students have filled in the correct answer space.

SAY: **Now place your marker under the next row. This is Sample D.**

Check to see that all students find Sample D.

SAY: **Listen to the last part of Takashi's letter. Read it silently to yourself as I read it aloud.**

Will you writing soon?
I want to know more about you.

Your friend,
Takashi

Look at the underlined word. Did Takashi use the right word? Should it be *write*, *writes*, or is the underlined word *Correct*

T34 © Steck-Vaughn Publishing Company

Primary 1 Intro, SV 7165-1

the way it is? Darken the circle for *the way Takashi should write the underlined word.*

Allow students time to choose and mark their answer.

SAY: **You should have darkened the circle for the** *first word*. **The sentence should read,** *Will you write soon*?

Check to see that all students have filled in the correct answer spaces.

Ask students if they have any questions.

SAY: **Look at the arrow with the words** *GO ON* **at the bottom of the page. This tells you to go to the next page and continue working on the test.**

SAY: **Now turn to page 58.**

Check to see that all students find page 58.

SAY: **Now we will continue the test. You will find more words and sentences that answer questions about stories you hear. Listen carefully to each story. Then choose your answer from the words and sentences given. Look at the picture under the title** *The Science Fair,* **while I read you a story about Pam.**

Check to see that all students find *The Science Fair*.

SAY: **Now listen carefully. Pam is going to make a project for the school's science fair. She is going to tell how seeds move from place to place. Now place your marker under the first row. Be sure to move your marker so you can see all the answer choices.**

Check to see that all students find item 5. Allow students time after each item to choose and mark their answer.

SAY: 5 **What should Pam do to find more information about how seeds move? Should she** *buy seeds from a store, find a library book about seeds,* **or** *go to a park*? **Darken the circle for** *what Pam should do to find more information about how seeds move.*

6 **Place your marker under the next row. What should Pam do before writing her science report? Should she** *list ways seeds move, plant some seeds,* **or** *glue seeds to paper*? **Darken the circle that tells what** *Pam should do first.*

SAY: **Listen to Pam's science report, titled** *Animals Help Seeds Move*. **Read it silently to yourself as I read it aloud.**

Check to see that all students find *Animals Help Seeds Move*.

SAY: *Animals Help Seeds Move*

Some animals help seeds move.
Birds pick up seeds to eat.
They may <u>dropping</u> *the seeds as they fly.*
I have a new dog.
The seeds grow where they fall on the ground.

Look at the arrow with the words *GO ON* **at the bottom of the page. This tells you to go to the next page and continue working on the test.**

SAY: **Now go to page 59.**

Check to see that all students find page 59.

SAY: **Place your marker under the first row.**

Check to see that all students find item 7. Allow students time after each item to choose and mark their answer.

SAY: 7 **Which sentence does not belong in the story? Is it** *Some animals help seeds move, Birds pick up seeds to eat,* **or** *I have a new dog*? **Darken the circle for the sentence that does** *not belong in the story.*

8 **Place your marker under the next row on the page. Look at the underlined word. How should Pam write this word? Should she write** *drops, drop,* **or is the underlined word** *Correct the way it is*? **Darken the circle for** *the way Pam should write the underlined word.*

SAY: **We will now continue the test. Now place your marker under the next row. Listen to the rest of Pam's science report. Read it silently to yourself as I read it aloud.**

Some seeds stick to the fur of animals.
They <u>dont</u> *fall off easily.*
The ends of the seeds are turned up.

SAY: **Now place your marker under the next row.**

Check to see that all students find item 9. Allow students time after each item to choose and mark their answer.

SAY: 9 **Look at the underlined word. How should Pam write this word? Should she write** *don't, do'nt,* **or is the underlined word** *Correct the way it is*? **Darken the circle for** *the way Pam should write the underlined word.*

10 **Place your marker under the next row. Pam wants to describe what the seed looks like. Which sentence is the best**

way for Pam to tell what the seed looks like? Should she write *The seed ends look sharp and look like a fishhook*, *The seed ends look sharp and like a fishhook*, or *The seed ends look like a sharp fishhook*? Darken the circle for the sentence that is *the best way for Pam to tell what the seed looks like.*

SAY: 11 Place your marker under the last row on the page. Pam used these words in her story: *seeds, stick*, and *sharp*. She wanted to look them up in the dictionary to make sure they were spelled correctly. Darken the circle for the word that would be *listed first in alphabetical (ABC) order in the dictionary.*

Look at the arrow with the words *GO ON* at the bottom of the page. This tells you to go to the next page and continue working on the test.

SAY: **Now turn to page 60.**

Check to see that all students find page 60.

SAY: **Now I will read you another story. Look at the picture under the title *The New Car*, while I read you a story about Mr. Lu.**

Check to see that all students find *The New Car*.

SAY: **Listen carefully to this story. Mr. Lu is going to sell his car. He wants to buy a new car. He is making a list of things he will look for in his new car. Now place your marker under the first row.**

Check to see that all students find item 12. Allow students time after each item to choose and mark their answer.

SAY: 12 **Which will not be on Mr. Lu's list? Will it be *a red car, a safe car*, or *wash the car*? Darken the circle for *what will not be on Mr. Lu's list.***
 13 **Place your marker under the last row on the page. What should Mr. Lu do to find more information about how safe a car is? Should he *talk to a car salesperson, drive a car*, or *look under a car*? Darken the circle for what Mr. Lu should do *to find more information about how safe a car is.***

Look at the arrow with the words *GO ON* at the bottom of the page. This tells you to go to the next page and continue working on the test.

SAY: **Now go to page 61.**

Check to see that all students find page 61.

SAY: **We will now continue the test. Place your marker under the first row, which shows Mr. Lu's list, *A Safe Car*.**

Check to see that all students find the list, *A Safe Car*.

SAY: **Listen to what Mr. Lu wrote on his list. Read it silently to yourself as I read it aloud.**

A Safe Car

The car should be very safe. It needs seat belts in the front and the back.

It must have new tires. The horn should honk. Very loudly for people to hear.

SAY: **Now place your marker under the next row.**

Check to see that all students find item 14. Allow students time after each item to choose and mark their answer.

SAY: 14 **Which group of words is not a complete sentence? Is it *The car should be very safe*, *It must have new tires*, or *Very loudly for people to hear*? Darken the circle beside the words that *do not make a complete sentence.***
 15 **Place your marker under the last row on the page. Mr. Lu wants to tell more about how the car should look. Should he write *The car will have two doors*, *I want a car I saw at the store*, or *It should be a new car*? Darken the circle for the words that tell *how Mr. Lu's car will look.***

Look at the arrow with the words *GO ON* at the bottom of the page. This tells you to go to the next page and continue working on the test.

SAY: **Now turn to page 62.**

Check to see that all students find page 62.

SAY: **Now listen to the rest of the story about Mr. Lu. Mr. Lu needs to sell his old car before he buys the new one. He wrote a description of his car to put in the newspaper. This is what he wrote. Read it silently to yourself as I read it aloud.**

Check to see that all students find *For Sale*.

SAY: ***For Sale***
 I <u>have</u> a car for sale.
 (1)
 It is in very good shape.

I need to sell it before Thursday, june 28.
                    (2)

SAY: **Now place your marker under the next row.**

Check to see that all students find item 16. Allow students time after each item to choose and mark their answer.

SAY: 16 **Look at the underlined word with the number *1* under it. Did Mr. Lu use the right word? Should he write *had, has*, or is it *Correct the way it is*? Darken the circle for *the way the underlined word should be written*.**
17 **Place your marker under the next row. Look at the underlined words with the number *2* under them. How should the words be written? Should they be written *thursday, june 28*, *Thursday, June 28* or is the group of words *Correct the way it is*? Darken the circle for *the way the underlined words should be written*.**
18 **Place your marker under the last row on the page. Which sentence will Mr. Lu probably write next? Will he write *Please call to find out more*, *The car is sold*, or *I want to buy a red car*? Darken the circle for *the sentence Mr. Lu will probably write next*.**

Look at the arrow with the words *GO ON* at the bottom of the page. This tells you to go to the next page and continue working on the test.

SAY: **Now go to page 63.**

Check to see that all students find page 63.

SAY: **In the last part of the test you will find words that are not spelled correctly. Listen carefully. I will read a sentence. Three of the words are listed as the answer choices. Find the word that is not spelled correctly. Now place your marker under the first row. This is Sample E.**

Check to see that all students find Sample E.

SAY: ***The play was overe (over) at four o'clock.* Darken the circle next to the word that is *not spelled correctly*.**

Allow students time to choose and mark their answer.

SAY: **You should have darkened the circle for the second word. The word *over* is not spelled with an *e* at the end.**

Check to see that all students have filled in the correct answer space. Ask students if they have any questions.

SAY: **Now you will find more words that are not spelled correctly. Place your marker under the next row.**

Check to see that all students find item 19. Allow students time after each item to choose and mark their answer.

SAY: 19 **Listen to this sentence. *The snake livz (lives) under the rock.* Darken the circle next to the word that is *not spelled correctly*.**
20 **Place your marker under the next row. *The pond is filld (filled) with fish.* Darken the circle next to the word that is *not spelled correctly*.**
21 **Place your marker under the next row. *I didn't mean what I sed (said).* Darken the circle next to the word that is *not spelled correctly*.**
22 **Place your marker under the next row. *Put your toyes (toys) away in your room.* Darken the circle next to the word that is *not spelled correctly*.**
23 **Place your marker under the next row. *Mother parkt (parked) close to the house.* Darken the circle next to the word that is *not spelled correctly*.**

SAY: **Now look at the top of the page. Find the next column. Place your marker under the first row.**

Check to see that all students find item 24. Allow students time after each item to choose and mark their answer.

SAY: 24 **Listen to this sentence. *This is the ende (end) of the line.* Darken the circle next to the word that is *not spelled correctly*.**
25 **Place your marker under the next row. *Liz told a funny storie (story).* Darken the circle next to the word that is *not spelled correctly*.**
26 **Place your marker under the next row. *Your fase (face) has dirt on it.* Darken the circle next to the word that is *not spelled correctly*.**
27 **Place your marker under the next row. *The boys splashd (splashed) in the water.* Darken the circle next to the word that is *not spelled correctly*.**
28 **Place your marker under the next row. *Max bought two brushs (brushes).* Darken the circle next to the word that is *not spelled correctly*.**
29 **Place your marker under the next row. *The prety (pretty) pink present is for***

Grandmother. Darken the circle next to the word that is *not spelled correctly.*

SAY: **Look at the stop sign at the bottom of the page. You have completed the Unit 7 Test. Make sure that you have carefully filled in your answer spaces and have erased any stray marks. Then put your pencils down.**

After the test has been scored, review the questions and answer choices with students. If students are having difficulty, provide them with additional practice.

Comprehensive Tests

Test 1: Word Recognition

Allow about 20 minutes for this test. Read items at a moderate, steady pace.

SAY: **Turn to Test 1 on page 64.**

Check to see that all students find Test 1.

SAY: **In the first part of this test, you will find words that begin with the same sounds as pictures. Place your marker under the first row, the one with the picture of the watch. This is <u>Sample A</u>. Now look at the words next to the picture. Darken the circle for the word that begins with the same sound as** *watch...watch.*

Allow students time to choose and mark their answer. Remind students that they were instructed to find the word that begins with the same sound as the picture *watch.*

SAY: **You should have darkened the circle for the last word,** *wait.* **The "w" in** *wait* **makes the same sound as the "w" in** *watch. Car, also,* **and** *chin* **are not correct because they do not have a "w" sound.**

Check to see that all students have filled in the correct answer space. Ask students if they have any questions.

SAY: **Now you will find more words that begin with the same sounds as pictures. Look carefully at the picture. Then choose your answer from the words given in the row.**

Now we will begin. Place your marker under the next row, the one with the picture of the girl behind the tree.

Check to see that all students find item 1. Allow students time after each item to choose and mark their answer.

SAY: 1 **Look at the picture of the girl behind the tree. Darken the circle for the word that begins with the same sound as** *hide...hide.*
 2 **Place your marker under the next row. Look at the picture of the bridge. Darken the circle for the word that begins with the same sounds as** *bridge...bridge.*
 3 **Place your marker under the next row. Look at the picture of the cherry. Darken the circle for the word that begins with the same sounds as** *cherry...cherry.*
 4 **Place your marker under the next row. Look at the picture of the boy swimming. Darken the circle for the word that begins with the same sounds as** *swim...swim.*
 5 **Place your marker under the next row. Look at the picture of the princess. Darken the circle for the word that begins with the same sounds as** *princess...princess.*

Look at the stop sign at the bottom of the page. You have finished this part of the test and should put your pencils down.

SAY: **Now look at the top of page 65.**

Check to see that all students find page 65.

SAY: **In the next part of the test, you will find words that end with the same sounds as pictures. Place your marker under the first row, the one with the picture of the flag. This is <u>Sample B</u>. Now look at the words next to the picture. Darken the circle for the word that ends with the same sound as** *flag...flag.*

Allow students time to choose and mark their answer. Remind students that they were instructed to find the word that ends with the same sound as the picture *flag.*

SAY: **You should have darkened the circle for the second word,** *hug.* **The "g" in** *hug* **makes the same sound as the "g" in** *flag. Cage* **and** *flower* **are not correct because they do not have a "g" sound.** *Garden* **is not correct because the "g" sound in** *garden* **is at the beginning of the word.**

Check to see that all students have filled in the correct answer space. Ask students if they have any questions.

SAY: **Now you will find more words that end with the same sounds as pictures. Look carefully at the picture. Then choose your answer from the words given in the row.**

Now we will begin. Place your marker under the next row, the one with the picture of the list.

Check to see that all students find item 6. Allow students time after each item to choose and mark their answer.

SAY:
6. Look at the picture of the list. Darken the circle for the word that ends with the same sounds as *list...list*.
7. Place your marker under the next row. Look at the picture of the park. Darken the circle for the word that ends with the same sounds as *park...park*.
8. Place your marker under the next row. Look at the picture of the well. Darken the circle for the word that ends with the same sound as *well...well*.
9. Place your marker under the next row. Look at the picture of the pond. Darken the circle for the word that ends with the same sounds as *pond...pond*.
10. Place your marker under the next row. Look at the picture of the tent. Darken the circle for the word that ends with the same sounds as *tent...tent*.

Look at the stop sign at the bottom of the page. You have finished this part of the test and should put your pencils down.

SAY: **Now turn to page 66.**

Check to see that all students find page 66.

SAY: **In the last part of the test, you will choose words that have the same sound as underlined letters in words. Place your marker under the first row, the one with the word *fine*. This is Sample C. Look at the underlined letter in *fine*. Darken the circle for the word that has the same sound as the underlined letter in *fine...fine*.**

Allow students time to choose and mark their answer.

SAY: **You should have darkened the circle for the word *side*. *Side* has the same sound as the underlined "i" in the word *fine*.**

Check to see that all students have filled in the correct answer space. Ask students if they have any questions.

SAY: **Now you will choose more words that have the same sound as underlined letters in words. Put your marker under the next row, the one with the word *baking*. Do numbers 11 through 19 just as we did Sample C. Look carefully at the underlined letter. Then choose your answer from the words given in the row. When you come to the stop sign at the bottom of the page, put your pencils down.**

Allow students time to choose and mark their answer.

SAY: **You have now completed Test 1. Make sure that you have carefully filled in your answer spaces and have erased any stray marks. Then put your pencils down.**

After the test has been scored, review the questions and answer choices with students. If students are having difficulty, provide them with additional practice.

Test 2: Reading Vocabulary

Allow about 25 minutes for this test. Read items at a moderate, steady pace.

SAY: **Turn to Test 2, Reading Vocabulary, on page 67.**

Check to see that all students find Test 2.

SAY: **In the first part of the test, you will find words that have the same or almost the same meaning as underlined words in sentences. Place your marker under the first sentence. This is Sample A. Read the sentence silently as I read it aloud. *He wore a large hat.* Now read the four words listed below the sentence: *tiny, big, funny, round*. Darken the circle next to the word that means the same or almost the same as *large*.**

Allow students time to choose and mark their answer.

SAY: **You should have darkened the circle next to the second word, *big*. *Big* means the same as *large*. *Tiny, funny,* and *round* are not correct because they do not mean the same as *large*.**

Check to see that all students have filled in the correct answer space. Ask students if they have any questions.

SAY: **Now you will find more words that mean the same or almost the same as underlined words in sentences. Place your marker under the next sentence. Do numbers 1 through 7 just as we did Sample A. Read each sentence and the four words listed. Then darken the circle next to the word that means the same or almost the same as the underlined word. When you come to the stop sign at the bottom of the page, put your pencils down. You may now begin.**

Review the questions and answer choices with

students. Discuss with the class why one answer is correct and the others are not correct. Also check to see that students have carefully filled in their answer spaces and have completely erased any stray marks.

SAY: **Now turn to page 68.**

Check to see that all students find page 68.

SAY: **In the next part of the test, you will find words with meanings that are the opposite or almost the opposite of underlined words in sentences. Place your marker under the first sentence. This is Sample B. Read the sentence silently as I read it aloud.** *I like this park.* **Now read the four words listed below the sentence:** *our, the, any, that.* **Darken the circle next to the word that means the opposite or almost the opposite of** *this.*

Allow students time to choose and mark their answer.

SAY: **You should have darkened the circle next to the last word,** *that. That* **means the opposite of** *this. Our, the,* **and** *any* **are not correct because they do not mean the opposite of** *this.*

Check to see that all students have filled in the correct answer space. Ask students if they have any questions.

SAY: **Now you will find more words that mean the opposite or almost the opposite of underlined words in sentences. Place your marker under the next sentence. Do numbers 8 through 14 just as we did Sample B. Read each sentence and the four words listed. Then darken the circle next to the word that means the opposite or almost the opposite of the underlined word. When you come to the stop sign at the bottom of the page, put your pencils down. You may now begin.**

Allow students time to choose and mark their answers.

SAY: **It is now time to stop. You have completed Test 2. Make sure that you have carefully filled in your answer spaces and have completely erased any stray marks. Then put your pencils down.**

After the test has been scored, review the questions and answer choices with students. If students are having difficulty, provide them with additional practice.

Test 3: Reading Comprehension

Allow about 30 minutes for this test. Read items at a moderate, steady pace.

SAY: **Turn to Test 3 on page 69.**

Check to see that all students find Test 3.

SAY: **In the first part of the test, you will find sentences that tell about pictures. Place your marker under the picture in the first row. This is Sample A. Now look at the sentences next to the picture. Darken the circle next to the sentence that tells what is happening in the picture.**

Allow students time to choose and mark their answer.

SAY: **You should have darkened the circle next to the second sentence,** *Father holds the baby.* **This sentence tells what is happening in the picture. The first sentence is not correct because Mother is not rocking the baby to sleep in the picture. The third sentence is not correct because Father is not reading to the baby in the picture. Only the second sentence tells about the picture.**

Check to see that all students have filled in the correct answer space. Ask students if they have any questions.

SAY: **Now you will practice finding more sentences that tell about pictures. Place your marker under the picture in the next row. Do numbers 1 through 4 just as we did Sample A. Look at each picture. Then read the sentences next to the picture. Darken the circle next to the sentence that tells what is happening in the picture. When you come to the stop sign at the bottom of the page, put your pencils down. You have about 8 minutes to complete this page. You may now begin.**

Allow students about 8 minutes to choose and mark their answers.

SAY: **Now turn to page 70.**

Check to see that all students find page 70.

SAY: **In the last part of the test, you will answer questions about stories that you read. Place your marker under the first row, the one that has the title,** *Working with Dad.* **This is Sample B. Read the story. Then read the questions and the answer choices. Darken the circle next to the correct answer.**

Allow students time to choose and mark their answer.

SAY: **You should have darkened the circle next to the third answer choice,** *Planting a garden.* **You can tell from the story that Terri and her** dad are planting and watering seeds for a garden. The first answer choice is not correct because in the story Terri and her dad water plant and water seeds, but they do not eat seeds. The second answer choice is not correct. In the last sentence Terri says that they will have good things to eat. This tells you that they were not watering flowers. The correct answer is the third answer choice.

Check to see that all students have filled in the correct answer space. Ask students if they have any questions.

SAY: **Now you will practice answering more questions about stories that you read. Place your marker under the next row, the one that has the title, _Marta's Special Day_. Do numbers 1 through 20 just as we did Sample B. Read each story. Then read the questions and the answer choices that follow. Darken the circle next to the correct answer. When you come to the arrow and the words _GO ON_ at the bottom of the page, continue working on the next page. When you come to the stop sign at the bottom of page 75, put your pencils down. You have about 20 minutes to complete the test. You may now begin.**

Allow students about 20 minutes to choose and mark their answers.

SAY: **It is now time to stop. You have completed Test 3. Make sure you have carefully filled in your answer circles and have completely erased any stray marks. Then put your pencils down.**

After the test has been scored, review the questions and answer choices with students. If students are having difficulty, provide them with additional practice.

Test 4: Math Concepts

Allow about 30 minutes for this test. Read items at a moderate, steady pace.

SAY: **Turn to Test 4 on page 76.**

Check to see that all students find Test 4.

SAY: **In this test, you will find pictures and numbers that answer math problems you hear. Place your marker under the first row, the one with the picture of the sailboats. This is Sample A. Now listen carefully. Darken the circle for the number that tells _exactly how many sailboats are shown in the picture._**

Allow students time to choose and mark their answer.

SAY: **You should have darkened the second circle for the number _6_. There are _six_ sailboats shown in the picture.**

Check to see that all students have filled in the correct answer space. Ask students if they have any questions.

SAY: **Now place your marker under the second row, the one with the numbers in the boxes. This is Sample B. Now look at the numbers in the boxes. Listen carefully. These numbers are counted by threes. Darken the circle for _the number that belongs in the empty box._**

Allow students time to choose and mark their answer.

SAY: **You should have darkened the third circle for the number _49_. When you count by threes, you count _forty-three, forty-six, forty-nine, fifty-two,_ and _fifty-five._**

Check to see that all students have filled in the correct answer space. Ask students if they have any questions.

SAY: **Now you will find more pictures and numbers that answer math problems you hear. Place your marker under the next row, the one with the picture of the vase and flowers.**

Check to see that all students find item 1. Allow students time after each item to choose and mark their answer. Say each item only once. Do <u>not</u> say the item numbers.

SAY: 1 **Darken the circle for the _flower that is seventh from the vase_...the flower that is seventh from the vase.**
2 **Place your marker under the next row. Which numeral names the <u>most</u> number of things? Darken the circle for the numeral which names _the most number of things._**
3 **Place your marker under the last row, the one with the crayons. Each bundle has ten crayons and there are some extra crayons. How many crayons are there altogether? Darken the circle for _the number of crayons altogether._**

Look at the arrow with the words _GO ON_ at the bottom of the page. This tells you to go to the next page and continue working on the test.

SAY: **Now look at page 77.**

Check to see that all students find page 77.

SAY: **Now we will continue with the test. Place your marker under the first row on the page.**

Check to see that all students find item 4. Allow students time after each item to choose and mark their answer. Say each item only once.

SAY: 4 Look at the numbers. Which numeral names the least number of things? Darken the circle for the numeral which names *the least number of things.*

5 Place your marker under the next row on the page. Look at the numbers. Which number is between thirty-three and fifty-one in value? Darken the circle for the number *between thirty-three and fifty-one in value.*

6 Place your marker under the next row. Darken the circle for the figure that has *two-thirds shaded...two-thirds shaded.*

7 Place your marker under the next row, the one with the numbers in boxes. These numbers are counted by fives. Darken the circle for *the number that belongs in the empty box.*

8 Place your marker under the last row on the page. Which number sentence is in the same fact family as 2 + 3 = 5? Darken the circle for the number sentence that is *in the same fact family as 2 + 3 = 5.*

Look at the arrow with the words *GO ON* at the bottom of the page. This tells you to go to the next page and continue working on the test.

SAY: Now turn to page 78. Place your marker under the first row, the one with the picture of the divided, shaded squares.

Check to see that all students find page 78. Check to see that all students find item 9. Allow students time after each item to choose and mark their answer. Say each item only once.

SAY: 9 Carefully look at each of the figures. Darken the circle for the figure that has *three-fourths shaded...three-fourths shaded.*

10 Place your marker under the next row, the one with the four clocks. Look at the clocks. Darken the circle for the clock that shows *nine o'clock...nine o'clock.*

11 Place your marker under the next row, the one with the pictures of coins. Darken the circle under the number that tells *the exact value of the coins.*

12 Place your marker under the last row on the page. Be sure to move your marker so you can see all of the answer choices. Look at the bus and the ruler. How long is the bus? Darken the circle for the number that tells *how long the bus is.*

Look at the arrow with the words *GO ON* at the bottom of the page. This tells you to go to the next page and continue working on the test.

SAY: Now look at page 79. Place your marker under the first row on the page, the one with the picture of the pencil and the paper clips.

Check to see that all students find page 79. Check to see that all students find item 13. Allow students time after each item to choose and mark their answer. Say each item only once.

SAY: 13 Look at the pencil and the paper clips. Darken the circle for the number that tells about how many paper clips long the pencil is.

14 Place your marker under the next row, the one with the calendar for November. Darken the circle for the date of *the second Friday in November.*

15 Place your marker under the next row, the one with the clocks. Darken the circle for the clock that shows *nine-thirty...nine-thirty.*

16 Place your marker under the last row on the page. Look at the shapes. Darken the circle under the set of shapes that show *a square and a triangle together... a square and a triangle together.*

SAY: Look at the arrow with the words *GO ON* at the bottom of the page. This tells you to go to the next page and continue working on the test.

SAY: Now turn to page 80.

Check to see that all students find page 80.

SAY: 17 Place your marker under the first row, the one with the large shape. Darken the circle for the number that tells *how many corners there are on this shape.*

18 Place your marker under the next row, the one with the picture of a folded piece of paper. A shape has been cut from this folded piece of paper. Darken the circle for the picture that shows *the shape that was cut from the paper.*

19 Place your marker under the next row, the one with the pattern of shapes. Be sure to move your marker so you can see the answer choices. Darken the circle for *the two shapes that come next in this pattern.*

20 Place your marker under the last row on the page. Look at the four items in the row. Darken the circle for the item that *is shaped like a rectangle.*

SAY: **It is time to stop. You have completed Test 4. Make sure that you have carefully filled in your answer spaces and have erased any stray marks. Then put your pencils down.**

After the test has been scored, review the questions and answer choices with students. If students are having difficulty, provide them with additional practice.

Test 5: Math Problems

Allow about 25 minutes for this test. Read items at a moderate, steady pace.

SAY: **Turn to Test 5 on page 81.**

Check to see that all students find Test 5.

SAY: **In this test, you will find pictures and numbers that answer math problems you hear and see in pictures. Place your marker under the first row, the one with the pictures of the kites. This is the <u>Sample</u>. You will mark the circle next to the correct answer choice. Now listen carefully. Anna saw thirteen kites flying high in the park. After a while, six kites got tangled in the trees. How many kites were still flying then? Anna saw thirteen kites flying in the park. Then six kites got tangled in the trees. Darken the circle next to the number sentence that shows *how to find the number of kites that were still flying*.**

Allow students time to choose and mark their answer.

SAY: **You should have darkened the circle for the number sentence, 13 − 6 = ☐. This sentence reads *thirteen minus six equals blank*, and is the correct answer. To find out how many kites were still flying after six kites got tangled in the trees, you would subtract the six kites from the thirteen kites that were once all flying.**

Check to see that all students have filled in the correct answer space. Ask students if they have any questions.

SAY: **Now you will find more pictures and numbers that answer math problems you hear and see in pictures. Place your marker under the next row, the one with the pictures of the starfish.**

Check to see that all students find item 1. Allow students time after each item to choose and mark their answer. Say each item only once. Do <u>not</u> say the item numbers.

SAY: 1 **Look at the picture. Listen to this story. Jake saw eight starfish on the beach during his vacation. Then he saw two more starfish. How many starfish did Jake see altogether? Darken the circle next to the number sentence that shows *how to find the number of starfish that Jake saw*.**

2 **Place your marker under the next row, the one with the picture of the flower. Make sure you move your marker so you can see all the answer choices. Darken the circle for the number sentence that best shows *what is happening in this picture*.**

3 **Place your marker under the next row. Look at the items in the row. Which is different from the others? Darken the circle for the item *that does not belong*.**

SAY: **Look at the arrow with the words *GO ON* at the bottom of the page. This tells you to turn to the next page and continue working on the test.**

SAY: **Now look at page 82.**

Check to see that all students find page 82.

SAY: **Now we will continue with the test. Place your marker under the first row, the one with the picture of the drinking glasses.**

Check to see that all students find item 4. Allow students time after each item to choose and mark their answer. Say each item only once. Do <u>not</u> say the item numbers.

SAY: 4 **Look at the pictures of the glasses. Now listen to this story. Aunt Clare made a pitcher of lemonade. She had eight glasses to fill. Some of the glasses were tall and some of the glasses were short. She filled six glasses and then found that the pitcher was empty. Darken the circle for the picture that shows *what happened in this story*.**

5 **Place your marker under the next row, the one with the numbers. Listen to this riddle about a number. I am thinking of a number that is more than eight and less than twenty. It has a nine in it. What number am I thinking of? It is more than eight, less than twenty, and has a nine in it. Darken the circle for *the number that I am thinking of*.**

6 **Place your marker under the next row. Lita has the amount of coins shown in the picture. How much more will she need to have a total of thirty-five cents? Darken the circle for the number that shows *how much more cents Lita will need to make thirty-five cents*.**

7. Place your marker under the last row on the page, the one with the pictures of the fruit. Look at the pictures of the fruit. Darken the circle for the picture that shows *which two fruits Diego could buy with exactly thirty-five cents.*

Look at the arrow with the words *GO ON* at the bottom of the page. This tells you to go to the next page and continue working on the test.

SAY: **Now look at page 83.**

Check to see that all students find page 83.

SAY: **Now we will continue with the test. Place your marker under the first row, the one with the pictures of the beads.**

Check to see that all students find item 8. Allow students time after each item to choose and mark their answer. Say each item only once. Do not say the item numbers.

SAY:
8. **Listen to this story. Eleanor is using beads to make a bracelet. She knows that she needs twelve beads to make the bracelet. She finds that she needs five more beads. How many beads does she have already? Darken the circle for the picture that shows *how many beads Eleanor has already*.**

9. **Place your marker under the next row. Look at the picture graph titled *Boxes of Seeds Jesse Sold*. This graph shows how many boxes of seeds Jesse sold for his scout troop. You will use this graph to answer questions 9 through 12. Look at the graph and listen carefully. What kind of seeds sold the most? Darken the circle for *the kind of seeds that sold the most*.**

10. **Place your marker under the next row. Darken the circle for *the number of boxes of vegetable seeds Jesse sold*.**

11. **Place your marker under the next row. Darken the circle for the number that tells *how many more boxes of flower seeds Jesse sold than herb seeds*.**

12. **Place your marker under the last row on the page. How many boxes of seeds did Jesse sell altogether? Darken the circle for *the number of boxes of seeds Jesse sold altogether*.**

SAY: **It is time to stop. You have completed Test 5. Make sure that you have carefully filled in your answer spaces and have erased any stray marks. Then put your pencils down.**

After the test has been scored, review the questions and answer choices with students. If students are having difficulty, provide them with additional practice.

Test 6: Math Procedures

Allow about 20 minutes for this test. Read items at a moderate, steady pace.

SAY: **Turn to Test 6 on page 84.**

Check to see that all students find Test 6.

SAY: **In this test, you will add or subtract numbers that answer math problems you hear or read. Place your marker under the first row, the one with the pictures of the leaves. This is Sample A. Now listen carefully. Jason collects leaves. Yesterday he went hiking through the woods near the lake. He found six oak leaves. Then he found five maple leaves. How many leaves did he find altogether? Darken the circle for the number that tells *how many leaves he found altogether*.**

Allow students time to choose and mark their answer.

SAY: **You should have darkened the circle for the number *11*. He found six leaves and then he found five leaves. If you add these together, 6 + 5 = *11*.**

Check to see that all students have filled in the correct answer space. Ask students if they have any questions.

SAY: **Now place your marker under the next row, the one with the numbers. This is Sample B. You are asked to subtract thirteen from sixty-eight. Look at the answer choices. The last answer choice is *NG*. *NG* means *Not Given*. If you add or subtract a problem and the answer is not among the answer choices, darken the circle for *NG*.**

Now work Sample B on your own.

Allow students time to choose and mark their answer.

SAY: **You should have darkened the circle for *NG*. Sixty-eight minus thirteen equals fifty-five. The correct answer is not listed in the answer choices.**

Check to see that all students have filled in the correct answer space. Ask students if they have any questions.

SAY: **Now you will add or subtract more numbers that answer math problems you hear or** read. Place your marker under the next row, the one with the pictures of the dolls.

Check to see that all students find item 1. Allow students time after each item to choose and mark their answer. Say each item only once. Do not say the item numbers.

SAY: 1 Listen to this story. Mia likes rag dolls. She has been collecting rag dolls for some time. She had nine rag dolls. For her birthday she received three rag dolls. How many rag dolls does she have now? She had nine rag dolls. She received three more rag dolls. Darken the circle for the number that tells *how many rag dolls Mia has altogether*.

2 Place your marker under the next row, the one with the pictures of the helicopter and the airplane. Ellie went to the airport. She saw six airplanes. She also saw five helicopters. How many more airplanes than helicopters did Ellie see? Ellie saw six airplanes and five helicopters. Darken the circle for the number that tells *how many more airplanes than helicopters Ellie saw at the airport*.

3 Place your marker under the next row, the one with the picture of the letters. Fumio wrote fifteen letters. He mailed ten of them. How many did he have left to mail? Fumio wrote fifteen letters and mailed ten. Darken the circle for the number that tells *how many more letters Fumio has left to mail*.

4 Place your marker under the last row on the page. Look at the shells on the plate. Rosa found seven shells on the beach today. How many will she have if six more shells are added to the plate? Darken the circle for the number that tells *how many shells there will be on the plate if six more shells are added*.

Look at the arrow with the words GO ON at the bottom of the page. This tells you to go to the next page and continue working on the test.

SAY: **Now look at page 85.**

Check to see that all students find page 85.

SAY: **Now we will continue with the test. Place your marker under the first row on the page.**

Check to see that all students find item 5. Allow students time after each item to choose and mark their answer. Say each item only once. Do not say the item numbers.

SAY: 5 Look at the amount of money. Mr. Lee had eighty cents. He bought a soda for sixty cents. How much money did he have left? Mr. Lee had eighty cents and bought a soda for sixty cents. Darken the circle for *the amount of money he has left*.

6 Place your marker under the next row. Now listen carefully. Darken the circle for the number that is *closest in value to forty-two plus thirty-seven*.

SAY: **Now you will add or subtract more numbers that answer math problems you read. You will do problems 7 through 9 on your own. Read each problem. Then find the correct answer given among the answer choices. If you cannot find the correct answer, darken the circle for *NG*. When you come to the stop sign at the bottom of the page, put your pencils down. You will have about 10 minutes to complete the test. You may now begin.**

Allow students 10 minutes to find and mark their answers.

SAY: **It is now time to stop. You have completed Test 6. Make sure that you have carefully filled in your answer spaces and have completely erased any stray marks. Then put your pencils down.**

After the test has been scored, review the questions and answer choices with students. If students are having difficulty, provide them with additional practice items.

Test 7: Language

Allow about 35 minutes for this test. Read items at a moderate, steady pace.

SAY: **Turn to Test 7, Language, on page 86.**

Check to see that all students find Test 7.

SAY: **In this test you will choose pictures that answer questions about stories you hear. Place your marker under the first row. This is Sample A. Now listen carefully. Forest Lane is an old country road. There is a covered bridge on Forest Lane that is only wide enough for one car to drive across at a time. Darken the circle for the picture that shows *the bridge on Forest Lane*.**

Allow students time to choose and mark their answer.

SAY: **You should have darkened the circle for the**

first picture. **The first picture shows a bridge that is only wide enough for one car to drive across at a time.**

Check to see that all students have filled in the correct answer space. Ask students if they have any questions.

SAY: **Now you will choose more pictures that answer questions about stories you hear. Listen carefully to each story. Then choose your answer from the pictures given in the row. Place your marker under the next row.**

Check to see that all students find item 1. Allow students time after each item to choose and mark their answer. Do <u>not</u> say the item numbers.

SAY: 1 **Listen to this poem:**
*We looked all around for Richard's toy bear.
We finally found it behind a _____ .*
Darken the circle for the picture that will *rhyme with the poem.*

2 **Place your marker under the next row. Sam and Rolando were walking in the woods one night. As they passed under a tree, Rolando felt something sticky on his face. He wiped his face to get it off. Darken the circle for the picture that shows** *what Rolando felt on his face.*

3 **Place your marker under the next row. Rudy the goldfish lives in a fishbowl. Once Rudy lived in a sparkling stream in the woods. There he liked to hang in the trees near the stream. Darken the circle for the picture that shows** *something that could not happen.*

4 **Place your marker under the last row on the page. Every morning before school, Lita eats a good breakfast. After breakfast, she always brushes her teeth. Next, she dresses and combs her hair. Then she is ready to walk to the school bus stop. Darken the circle for the picture that shows** *what Lita does first each morning.*

Look at the arrow with the words *GO ON* **at the bottom of the page. This tells you to go to the next page and continue working on the test.**

SAY: **Now go to page 87.**

Check to see that all students find page 87.

SAY: **In this part of the test you will answer questions about stories you hear. Listen carefully to the story and questions. Then choose your answer from the words and sentences given. Place your marker under the first row. Be sure to move your marker so you can see all the answer choices. This is** <u>Sample B</u>.

Check to see that all students find <u>Sample B</u>.

SAY: **Look at the picture under the title,** *A Favorite Holiday,* **while I read you a story about Angie. Now listen carefully.**

Angie's teacher has asked the class to write a story telling about their favorite holiday. Angie's favorite holiday is the Fourth of July. What idea will Angie not use in her story? Is it *Go on a picnic, Open presents,* **or** *Watch fireworks*? **Darken the circle under the idea Angie** *will not use in her story.*

Allow students time to choose and mark their answer.

SAY: **You should have darkened the circle for the second answer,** *Open presents.* **Most people do not open presents on the Fourth of July.**

Check to see that all students have filled in the correct answer space.

SAY: **Now place your marker under the next row. This is** <u>Sample C</u>.

Check to see that all students find <u>Sample C</u>.

SAY: **Listen carefully to the beginning of Angie's story. Read it silently to yourself as I read it out loud.**

*I like the Fourth of July best.
My family and I like to watch the parade.
After the parade, we go to the park.
To have a picnic.*

Which group of words is not a complete sentence? Is it *I like the Fourth of July best, After the parade, we go to the park,* **or** *To have a picnic*? **Darken the circle next to the words that** *do not make a complete sentence.*

Allow students time to choose and mark their answer.

SAY: **You should have darkened the circle for the last group of words.** *To have a picnic* **is not a complete sentence.**

Check to see that all students have filled in the correct answer space.

SAY: **Now place your marker under the next row. This is** <u>Sample D</u>.

Check to see that all students find <u>Sample D</u>.

SAY: **Listen to the last part of Angie's story. Read it silently to yourself as I read it out loud.**

*We <u>watches</u> the fireworks at night.
The colors light up the sky.*

Look at the underlined word. Did Angie use the right word? Should she write *watch*, *watching*, or is the underlined word *Correct the way it is*? Darken the circle for *the way Angie should write the underlined word*.

Allow students time to choose and mark their answer.

SAY: **You should have darkened the circle for the first word, *watch*. This is the correct word to use. The sentence should read *We watch the fireworks at night*.**

Check to see that all students have filled in the correct answer spaces. Ask students if they have any questions.

SAY: **Look at the arrow with the words *GO ON* at the bottom of the page. This tells you to go to the next page and continue working on the test.**

SAY: **Now turn to page 88.**

Check to see that all students find page 88.

SAY: **Now we will continue the test. You will find more words and sentences that answer questions about stories you hear. Listen carefully to each story. Then choose your answer from the words and sentences given. Look at the picture under the title *The Swimming Party* while I read you a story about Mike.**

Check to see that all students find *The Swimming Party*.

SAY: **Now listen carefully. Mike is having a swimming party at his house. He is sending invitations to all of his friends. Place your marker under the first row. Be sure to move your marker so you can see all the answer choices.**

Check to see that all students find item 5. Allow students time after each item to choose and mark their answer. Do <u>not</u> say the item numbers.

5 **What information will Mike not put in his invitations? Is it *the time the party begins*, *the size of the pool*, or *his house number and street name*? Darken the circle next to the information Mike *will not put in the invitation*.**

6 **Place your marker under the next row. Mike used these words in his invitation: *when, wish, water*. He wanted to look them up in a dictionary to make sure he spelled them correctly. Darken the circle for the word that would be *listed first in alphabetical (ABC) order in the dictionary*.**

SAY: **Now place your marker under the next row. Look at the beginning of an invitation Mike wrote. Read it silently to yourself as I read it out loud.**

Check to see that all students find the beginning of Mike's invitation.

SAY: **Dear Sal,**

*I am having a swimming party.
It will be this <u>Friday, August 19</u>.*
　　　　　　　　　(1)
*Come to my house at 359 Pine Road.
<u>We will much fun have.</u>*
　　　　　(2)

SAY: **Now you will answer some questions. Place your marker under the next row.**

Check to see that all students find item 7. Allow students time after each item to choose and mark their answer. Do <u>not</u> say the item numbers.

7 **Listen carefully. Look at the underlined words with the number *1* under them. How should Mike write these words? Should he write *friday, august 19*, *friday, August 19*, or is the group of the underlined words *Correct the way it is*? Darken the circle for the way Mike should *write the underlined words*.**

8 **Place your marker under the last row on the page. Look at the underlined sentence with the number *2* under it. How should Mike write this sentence? Should he write *We will have much fun*, *We will have fun much*, or is the underlined sentence *Correct the way it is*? Darken the circle for the way Mike should *write the underlined sentence*.**

Look at the arrow with the words *GO ON* at the bottom of the page. This tells you to go to the next page and continue working on the test.

SAY: **Now look at page 89.**

Check to see that all students find page 89.

© Steck-Vaughn Publishing Company

SAY: **We will now continue the test. Place your marker under the first row. Listen to the rest of Mike's invitation. Read it silently to yourself as I read it out loud.**

Check to see that all students find the rest of Mike's invitation.

SAY: *You need to bring a swimsuit.*
　　　　　　　(1)
I hope to see you.
Let me know if you arent coming.
　　　　　　　　　　(2)

Your friend,
Mike

SAY: **Now you will answer some questions. Place your marker under the next row.**

Check to see that all students find item 9. Allow students time after each item to choose and mark their answer. Do not say the item numbers.

SAY: 9 **Look at the underlined word with the number *1* under it. Did Mike use the right word? Should he write *needing*, *needed*, or is it *Correct the way it is*? Darken the circle for the way *the underlined word should be written*.**

10 **Place your marker under the next row. Look at the underlined word with the number *2* under it. Did Mike use the right word? Should he write *aren't*, *are'nt* or is it *Correct the way it is*? Darken the circle for *the way the underlined word should be written*.**

SAY: **Now I will read another story. Look at the picture under the title *Around Town*.**

Check to see that all students find *Around Town*.

SAY: **Now listen as I read you a story about Tia. Tia is writing a report about the things to see and do in her town. She put a Table of Contents at the front of her report. Read it silently to yourself as I read it out loud. Chapter 1 is called *What to See* and begins on page 3. Chapter 2 is called *What to Do* and begins on page 10. Chapter 3 is called *Where to Eat* and begins on page 17. Chapter 4 is called *Special Activities* and begins on page 26. Now place your marker under the next row.**

Check to see that all students find item 11. Allow students time after each item to choose and mark their answer. Do not say the item numbers.

SAY: 11 **Look at the Table of Contents again. Would Tia write about a place to eat pizza on page *10*, page *17*, or page *26*? Darken the circle for the page Tia will use to write about *a place to eat pizza*.**

12 **Place your marker under the last row on the page. Look at the Table of Contents again. What chapter would Tia use to write about a place that has dinosaur bones? Would she use Chapter *1*, Chapter *2*, or Chapter *3*? Darken the circle for the chapter Tia would use to write about a place *that has dinosaur bones*.**

Look at the arrow with the words *GO ON* at the bottom of the page. This tells you to go to the next page and continue working on the test.

SAY: **Now turn to page 90.**

Check to see that all students find page 90.

SAY: **Now we will now continue the test. Place your marker under the first row. Listen to what Tia wrote in her report. Read it to yourself silently as I read it out loud.**

Check to see that all students find Tia's report.

SAY: *In my town, you can visit a cave.*
A train takes you under the ground.
A man tells you about the cave.
As you walk on a wide path.

SAY: **Now place your marker under the next row.**

Check to see that all students find item 13. Allow students time to choose and mark their answer. Do not say the item number.

13 **Which group of words is not a complete sentence? Is it *A train takes you under the ground*, *A man tells you about the cave*, or *As you walk on a wide path*? Darken the circle next to the group of words that *does not make a complete sentence*.**

SAY: **Now listen to what Tia wrote next in her report. Read it silently to yourself as I read it aloud.**

Check to see that all students find the rest of Tia's report.

SAY: *You can also go to the library.*
Each Tuesday they have a story time.
　　　(1)
Someone reads a story to the children.
　　(2)
Sometimes they have a puppet play.

SAY: **Now place your marker under the next row.**

Check to see that all students find item 14. Allow students time after each item to choose and mark their answer. Do not say the item numbers.

SAY: 14 **Look at the underlined word with the number *1* under it. How should Tia write this word? Should she use a capital letter? Darken the circle for the answer that shows how Tia should write** *the underlined word.*

15 **Place your marker under the last row on the page. Look at the underlined words with the number *2* under them. How should Tia write these words? Should she write *Someone reading, Someone read*, or is the group of words *Correct the way it is*? Darken the circle for the answer that shows how Tia should write** *the underlined words.*

Look at the arrow with the words *GO ON* at the bottom of the page. This tells you to go to the next page and continue working on the test.

SAY: **Now look at page 91.**

Check to see that all students find page 91.

SAY: **Now we will continue the test. I will read another story. Look at the picture under the title *Summer Fun* as I read you a story about Bert.**

Check to see that all students find *Summer Fun*.

SAY: **It was the beginning of the school year. The teacher asked the students to write a story about what they did during the summer. Bert had gone to Camp Lakota and learned how to sail a boat. Bert decided to write about sailing the boat.**

SAY: **Now you will answer a question. Place your marker under the first row.**

Check to see that all students find item 16. Allow students time to choose and mark their answer. Do not say the item number.

SAY: 16 **Why is Bert writing a story? Is it *to tell his friend how to sail, to tell what he did during the summer,* or *to tell what he did at camp*? Darken the circle next to the words that tell** *why Bert is writing a story.*

SAY: **Now listen to what Bert wrote in his story, *Learning to Sail*. Read it silently to yourself as I read it aloud.**

Check to see that all students find *Learning to Sail*.

SAY: *Learning to Sail*

I learned to sail a boat at camp.
We ate hot dogs.
First, you have to raise the sails.
The wind fills the sails.

SAY: **Now you will answer some questions. Place your marker under the next row.**

Check to see that all students find item 17. Allow students time after each item to choose and mark their answer. Do not say the item numbers.

SAY: 17 **What sentence will Bert probably write next? Is it *The wind makes the boat move, The camp is beside a lake*, or *The boat is big*? Darken the circle next to the sentence that Bert** *will probably write next.*

18 **Place your marker under the last row on the page. Which sentence does not belong in the story? Is it *I learned to sail a boat at camp, We ate hot dogs*, or *First, you have to raise the sails*? Darken the circle next to the sentence that does not belong in the story.**

Look at the arrow with the words *GO ON* at the bottom of the page. This tells you to go to the next page and continue working on the test.

SAY: **Now turn to page 92.**

Check to see that all students find page 92.

SAY: **Now I will read you the next part of Bert's story. Read it silently to yourself as I read it aloud.**

Check to see that all students find the rest of Bert's story.

SAY: *Sometimes the wind does not blow.*
Guess what happens then
                         (1)
The boat will not move.
Mr. sanchez, the camp leader, must
       (2)
come get you.

SAY: **Now you will answer some questions. Place your marker under the first row.**

Check to see that all students find item 19. Allow students time after each item to choose and mark their answer. Do not say the item numbers.

SAY: 19 **Look at the underlined word with the number *1* under it. Which punctuation mark should Bert write at the end this sentence? Should he write a period, a question mark, or an exclamation point? Darken the circle for *the punctuation mark Bert should write at the end of the word.***

20 **Place your marker under the last row on the page. Look at the underlined words with the number *2* under them. How should Bert write these words? Where should he use capital letters? Darken the circle for the answer that shows *how Bert should write these underlined words.***

Look at the arrow with the words *GO ON* at the bottom of the page. This tells you to go to the next page and continue working on the test.

SAY: **Now look at page 93.**

Check to see that all students find page 93.

SAY: **In the last part of the test you will find words that are not spelled correctly. Listen carefully. I will read a sentence. Three of the words are listed as the answer choices. Find the word that is not spelled correctly. Now place your marker under the first row. This is <u>Sample E</u>.**

Check to see that all students find <u>Sample E</u>.

SAY: **Listen carefully. *Mr. Jones read two storys (stories) to the class.* Darken the circle next to the word that is *not spelled correctly*.**

Allow students time to choose and mark their answer.

SAY: **You should have darkened the circle for the third word. The word *stories* is not spelled with a "ys" at the end. The word should be spelled *s–t–o–r–i–e–s*.**

Check to see that all students have filled in the correct answer space. Ask students if they have any questions.

SAY: **Now you will find more words that are not spelled correctly. Place your marker under the next row.**

Check to see that all students find item 21. Allow students time after each item to choose and mark their answer. Do not say the item numbers.

SAY: 21 **Listen carefully. *We packt (packed) our bags for the trip.* Darken the circle next to the word that is *not spelled correctly*.**

22 **Place your marker under the next row. *Please give hir (her) a turn.* Darken the circle next to the word that is *not spelled correctly*.**

23 **Place your marker under the next row. *The girl made three wishs (wishes).* Darken the circle next to the word that is *not spelled correctly*.**

24 **Place your marker under the next row. *The children playd (played) in the sun.* Darken the circle next to the word that is *not spelled correctly*.**

25 **Place your marker under the next row. *Did you win first prise (prize)?* Darken the circle next to the word that is *not spelled correctly*.**

SAY: **Now look at the top of the page. Find the next column. Place your marker under the first row.**

Check to see that all students find item 26.

26 **Listen carefully. *How many dayes (days) until my birthday?* Darken the circle next to the word that is *not spelled correctly*.**

27 **Place your marker under the next row. *Rosa was carful (careful) not to wake her father.* Darken the circle next to the word that is *not spelled correctly*.**

28 **Place your marker under the next row. *Please pick up your toyes (toys) before you leave.* Darken the circle next to the word that is *not spelled correctly*.**

29 **Place your marker under the next row. *My frend (friend) is riding his bike.* Darken the circle next to the word that is *not spelled correctly*.**

30 **Place your marker under the next row. *Maria fell and bumped her noze (nose).* Darken the circle next to the word that is *not spelled correctly*.**

31 **Place your marker under the last row on the page. *The teacher calld (called) your name.* Darken the circle next to the word that is *not spelled correctly*.**

SAY: **Look at the stop sign at the bottom of the page. You have completed Test 7. Make sure that you have carefully filled in your answer spaces and have erased any stray marks. Then put your pencils down.**

After the test has been scored, review the questions and answer choices with students. If students are having difficulty, provide them with additional practice.

UNIT 1 Word Recognition

Lesson 1: Recognizing Beginning Sounds

Sample

-0 A+ Derek

name	know	mountain	your
○	○	●	○

STOP

1

club	water	between	rub
○	○	●	○

2

house	where	another	wagon
○	●	○	○

3

nice	snap	kite	bees
○	●	○	○

4

stand	river	bird	mix
○	○	○	●

5

broom	kitten	their	clock
○	○	○	●

STOP

Primary 1

Lesson 2: Recognizing Ending Sounds

Sample

| monkey ● | ten ○ | yellow ○ | home ○ |

1

| eight ● | feather ○ | before ○ | luck ○ |

2

| mouse ○ | rake ○ | farm ● | what ○ |

3

| shelf ○ | wish ○ | under ● | clean ○ |

4

| lamp ● | money ○ | just ○ | eat ○ |

5

| scarf ○ | lazy ○ | bank ● | wear ○ |

Primary 1

Lesson 3: Recognizing Vowel Sounds

Sample

time
- ○ animal
- ○ whistle
- ● shine
- ○ hill

1

later
- ○ piano
- ○ roar
- ○ arrow
- ● grade

2

popping
- ○ old
- ○ torn
- ● knob
- ● office

3

being
- ○ mend
- ● eagle
- ○ vest
- ○ web

4

jungle
- ○ would
- ● puzzle
- ○ rule
- ○ blue

5

picture
- ○ tire
- ○ fight
- ● simple
- ○ ride

6

over
- ○ lost
- ● broken
- ○ now
- ○ come

7

nest
- ○ green
- ○ leaf
- ○ she
- ● penny

8

back
- ○ place
- ○ table
- ● travel
- ○ rain

9

about
- ○ pocket
- ○ rock
- ○ town
- ● rainbow

Primary 1

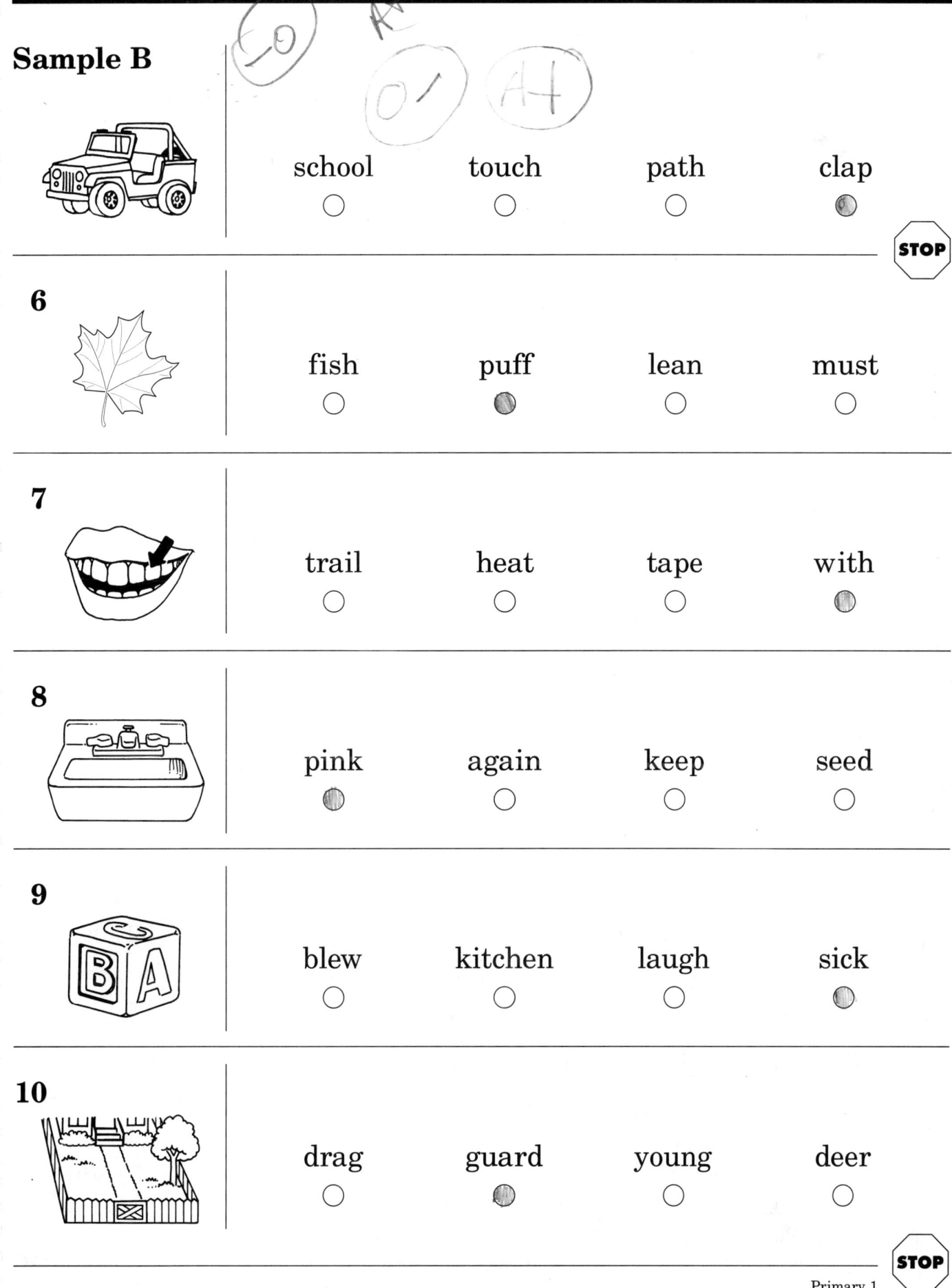

Sample C

b<u>ea</u>n
- ○ send
- ○ little
- ○ head
- ● leak

11 pl<u>a</u>te
- ○ have
- ● stage
- ○ watch
- ○ arm

12 h<u>o</u>pped
- ○ orange
- ○ worn
- ○ golden
- ● locking

13 m<u>e</u>ss
- ○ steam
- ● kettle
- ○ between
- ○ cream

14 h<u>u</u>nting
- ● tunnel
- ○ tool
- ○ could
- ○ sour

15 chi<u>c</u>ken
- ○ sight
- ● ticket
- ○ rice
- ○ fire

16 <u>o</u>nly
- ○ sock
- ○ cost
- ○ soil
- ● notice

17 sh<u>ou</u>t
- ○ glove
- ● crowd
- ○ zoo
- ○ purse

18 h<u>oo</u>d
- ○ pool
- ● should
- ○ cone
- ○ bounce

19 gl<u>a</u>nce
- ○ brave
- ○ part
- ● quack
- ○ garden

Primary 1

6

UNIT 2 Reading Vocabulary

Lesson 4: Matching Words with Similar Meanings

Sample

Put the flowers on the table.
- ○ Hold
- ○ Place
- ○ See
- ○ Take

1 Did you choose a song?
- ○ lose
- ○ play
- ○ pick
- ○ sing

2 It was a small rabbit.
- ○ old
- ○ white
- ○ fat
- ○ little

3 Petey did a good job.
- ○ work
- ○ dance
- ○ story
- ○ name

4 JoAnn was feeling scared.
- ○ lucky
- ○ afraid
- ○ better
- ○ lost

5 My shoes are beside the bed.
- ○ behind
- ○ under
- ○ by
- ○ above

6 Did you see the stars last night?
- ○ day
- ○ noon
- ○ today
- ○ evening

7 She wants to keep that card.
- ○ save
- ○ sign
- ○ read
- ○ mail

Primary 1

Lesson 5: Matching Words with Opposite Meanings

Sample
Please close the <u>back</u> door.
- ○ front
- ○ center
- ○ broken
- ○ closet

STOP

1. Did the team <u>win</u> their game?
   - ○ see
   - ○ play
   - ○ lose
   - ○ watch

2. Look at the <u>top</u> row.
   - ○ crowded
   - ○ last
   - ○ middle
   - ○ bottom

3. This game is <u>simple</u>.
   - ○ fun
   - ○ strange
   - ○ easy
   - ○ hard

4. <u>Whisper</u> your secret to me.
   - ○ Tell
   - ○ Shout
   - ○ Show
   - ○ Say

5. That magic trick <u>always</u> works.
   - ○ often
   - ○ soon
   - ○ never
   - ○ sometimes

6. This towel is <u>wet</u>.
   - ○ soft
   - ○ dry
   - ○ old
   - ○ damp

7. Please arrive <u>early</u>.
   - ○ today
   - ○ soon
   - ○ now
   - ○ late

STOP

Primary 1

Unit 2 Test

Sample A
Don't <u>hurt</u> yourself.
- ○ help
- ○ scare
- ○ harm
- ○ lose

1 Move <u>forward</u> slowly.
- ○ ahead
- ○ away
- ○ over
- ○ back

2 It is a <u>beautiful</u> picture.
- ○ torn
- ○ new
- ○ dark
- ○ pretty

3 Let's <u>race</u> to the corner.
- ○ ride
- ○ step
- ○ run
- ○ go

4 Put the cans in this brown <u>bag</u>.
- ○ sack
- ○ envelope
- ○ paper
- ○ basket

5 <u>Sign</u> your name on this line.
- ○ Say
- ○ Know
- ○ Write
- ○ Color

6 Which toy is <u>missing</u>?
- ○ last
- ○ broken
- ○ new
- ○ gone

7 What time did the movie <u>end</u>?
- ○ start
- ○ finish
- ○ run
- ○ break

Sample B
Do you need <u>more</u> money?
- ○ some
- ○ less
- ○ any
- ○ my

---

8 The water is too <u>cold</u>.
- ○ hot
- ○ high
- ○ rough
- ○ dirty

---

9 Can you <u>fix</u> my sled?
- ○ paint
- ○ sell
- ○ pull
- ○ break

---

10 That rope is too <u>long</u>.
- ○ heavy
- ○ short
- ○ weak
- ○ thick

---

11 Dad wants to <u>sell</u> his car.
- ○ buy
- ○ paint
- ○ drive
- ○ wash

---

12 <u>Push</u> the door open.
- ○ Keep
- ○ Pull
- ○ Hold
- ○ Leave

---

13 This is a <u>full</u> cup.
- ○ metal
- ○ empty
- ○ tea
- ○ broken

---

14 Jesse's dog is <u>lost</u>.
- ○ sick
- ○ found
- ○ brown
- ○ sleeping

Primary 1

UNIT 3 Reading Comprehension

Lesson 6: Understanding Sentences

Sample

- ○ Her new coat has a furry collar.
- ○ Dee Ann is reading the book.
- ○ The dog is under the desk.

1

- ○ Mr. Salinas lives on my street.
- ○ Corn and beans grow in the garden.
- ○ Mr. Salinas works in his garden.

2

- ○ Becky pours milk for her cat.
- ○ The cat is playing.
- ○ Becky has a cat named Whiskers.

3

- ○ She is on vacation.
- ○ Keiko is mailing a letter.
- ○ Keiko likes to draw pictures.

4

- ○ The rabbit is wearing a hat.
- ○ The hat is too big for the rabbit.
- ○ Rabbits live in that field.

Primary 1

Lesson 7: Reading Stories

Sample
Our Toys
We each have a toy.
Maria has a red car.
Ron's car is blue.
My car is yellow.

What color is Ron's car?
○ Red
○ Blue
○ Yellow

What did Danny learn?

Danny likes to help his family. He is only four years old. He thinks he can do things his big brother can do. He wanted to help his dad. His dad was painting the house. His dad gave Danny paint and a brush.

Danny got paint all over his clothes. Dad said, "You will do better when you are five." Danny said, "I don't want to paint any more. I want to have some fun." Dad laughed.

1. **Why did Danny want to paint the house?**
   ○ He was a good painter.
   ○ He wanted to help his family.
   ○ He did not like the color of the house.

2. **What happened to Danny's clothes?**
   ○ He tore them.
   ○ He washed them.
   ○ He got paint on them.

3. **What might happen next in the story?**
   ○ Dad will tell Danny to finish painting.
   ○ Danny will go out to play.
   ○ Danny will wash his clothes.

4. **This story was written to—**
   ○ make readers laugh.
   ○ teach readers how to paint.
   ○ make readers want to paint.

Primary 1

Tess and Her Blocks

Tess has a set of blocks. Her blocks are red, blue, and green. She builds many things with her blocks. One day she built a blue block house. Another day she built a car of red blocks. Sometimes her block buildings fall down. Then she feels sad. She has to start building all over again.

5 What did Tess build with the blue blocks?
- ○ A car
- ○ An airplane
- ○ A house

6 What did Tess build with red blocks?
- ○ A house
- ○ A car
- ○ A tower

7 How does Tess feel when the blocks fall?
- ○ Unhappy
- ○ Tired
- ○ Angry

8 What is this story **mainly** about?
- ○ Building houses
- ○ Playing with blocks
- ○ Sad things

Skippy

We have a new dog at our house. His name is Skippy. He is two years old. My sister and I like to play with Skippy. We throw a ball, and he brings it back. We take him for walks on our street. Skippy barks when he is hungry. I put food in his bowl. My sister gives him cool water. We take good care of Skippy.

9 **How old is Skippy?**

○ Two months old

○ One year old

○ Two years old

10 **When does Skippy bark?**

○ When he goes for a walk

○ When he wants food

○ When he wants water

11 **Which of these is another good name for this story?**

○ "How to Take Care of a Dog"

○ "Our New Pet"

○ "Fun with Dogs"

12 **How do the children feel about Skippy?**

○ They love him.

○ They think he barks too much.

○ They are afraid of him.

Lucy's Gloves

Lucy couldn't find her gloves. She looked in her desk. They were not there. She looked on the floor. They were not there. Her teacher asked her what was wrong.

"I can't find my new gloves. My grandmother made them for me. They are my favorite colors, green and white."

"Let's look for Lucy's gloves," said the teacher.

All the students searched for Lucy's gloves, but no one could find them. Lucy was very unhappy.

When it was time to go home, the children put on their coats and gloves. Lucy put her hands in her pockets. She hoped her hands would stay warm on her way home. Then she started to smile. Now she knew where her gloves were!

13 Where was Lucy?
- ○ At school
- ○ At home
- ○ At her grandmother's house

14 Lucy liked her gloves because—
- ○ they fit her hands well.
- ○ they were very warm.
- ○ they were green and white.

15 Where did Lucy find her gloves?
- ○ In her desk
- ○ In her coat pockets
- ○ On the floor

16 What will most likely happen next in the story?
- ○ Lucy will put on her gloves and walk home.
- ○ Lucy will walk home with her hands in her pockets.
- ○ Lucy will ask her grandmother to make her more gloves.

What do you know about bread?

When you think of bread, what comes to mind? Do you think of a fresh loaf of white bread? Perhaps you picture a nice loaf of wheat bread. If you lived in another country, you might have a very different idea of bread. A boy or girl in Mexico would think of tortillas. These are flat, round breads made from corn or flour. People in India would think of *chappatis*. These are heavy pieces of round bread that are fried.

Bread is one of the most important foods. It is eaten more than any other food. It is also eaten in more places than any other food.

Bread has been an important food for a very long time. The first bread was made about 12,000 years ago. People in the Middle East used the seeds of wild plants to make flour. They mixed the flour with water and then baked it on hot rocks.

Later, people learned how to plant seeds to grow their own wheat. People in Egypt learned that if they added yeast to the flour and water, it would make the bread rise.

For hundreds of years, bread was made in the same way. But in time people wanted a light bread. They learned that if flour was sifted through cloth, the rough pieces could be taken out. Then they would have white flour. From white flour soft, white bread could be made. For many years only rich people could buy white bread. Today many people like whole wheat bread better than white bread. We know that the rough pieces in flour are good for us.

17 What does the word *chappatis* in this story mean?

- ○ Loaves of soft, white bread
- ○ Flat, round bread made of corn
- ○ Heavy pieces of fried bread
- ○ Round loaves of wheat bread

18 Who first added yeast to bread?

- ○ People in the Middle East
- ○ Egyptians
- ○ Germans
- ○ Rich people

19 Why did people sift flour through cloth?

- ○ To take out the rough pieces of flour
- ○ To make the flour cleaner
- ○ To make the bread rise
- ○ So that they would not have to knead the dough

20 Which words in the story tell what people used to make the first flour?

- ○ ...the seeds of wild plants...
- ○ ...their own wheat...
- ○ ...soft, white bread...
- ○ ...about 12,000 years ago...

21 Why did white bread cost so much at first?

- ○ White flour was harder to make.
- ○ White flour was made from gold.
- ○ White flour did not stay fresh long.
- ○ White flour kept the yeast from rising.

22 This story was written to—

- ○ make readers laugh.
- ○ teach readers something.
- ○ tell about a person.
- ○ tell readers how to make something.

STOP

Primary 1

Unit 3 Test

Sample A

- ○ The girl is watching a bird.
- ○ It is raining very hard.
- ○ The girl is planting flowers.

1

- ○ I like to march in a parade.
- ○ The clown rides the elephant.
- ○ I am having a birthday party.

2

- ○ The queen is dancing with the king.
- ○ A fire is burning down the castle.
- ○ The queen is leaving the castle.

3

- ○ A police car is at the corner.
- ○ Many children are inside the bus.
- ○ I like my teacher.

4

- ○ Jesse cannot reach the book.
- ○ I have a new book.
- ○ Jesse is reading a book.

Primary 1

Sample B
Playing

Max throws the ball. Sue Lin hits the ball. James chases the ball.

Who hits the ball?
○ Max
○ Sue Lin
○ James

Rosa's Good Deed

One day Rosa found a baby bird in the yard. There was no nest nearby. There was no mother bird.

Rosa picked up the tiny bird. She made a nest for it in a shoe box. She fed it with an eyedropper.

She kept the bird for three weeks. The bird grew strong.

Rosa took the shoe box outside. The bird flew to a nearby tree. It began to sing. Rosa knew that her bird would be fine.

1 Where did Rosa find the bird?
   ○ In a nest
   ○ In the park
   ○ In the yard

2 Rosa took care of the baby bird for—
   ○ one day.
   ○ three weeks.
   ○ two months.

3 Rosa made a nest for the bird in—
   ○ a drawer in her room.
   ○ a shoe box.
   ○ a bush.

4 Why did the bird fly out of the shoe box?
   ○ It was ready to take care of itself.
   ○ It saw its mother.
   ○ It wanted to hide.

The Largest Land Animal

Have you ever seen an elephant? The elephant has a very long nose. It is called a trunk. An elephant's trunk weighs about 300 pounds. Elephants can use their trunk to smell. Sometimes they can smell danger in the air. Elephants use their trunk to hold things, too. They can hold up to 600 pounds. The trunk works almost like a hand.

Elephants use their trunk to reach food. Their trunk helps them *grasp* leaves high up in trees. They pull grasses from the ground. Elephants use their trunk in many ways. Do you wish you had a trunk?

5 The story says that elephants can smell—
- ○ leaves.
- ○ danger.
- ○ grasses.

6 What is this story mainly about?
- ○ What elephants eat
- ○ What elephants can smell
- ○ How elephants use their trunks

7 How many pounds can elephants hold with their trunks?
- ○ 200
- ○ 300
- ○ 600

8 What does the word *grasp* in this story mean?
- ○ Point to
- ○ Take hold of
- ○ Use in many ways

Tree Rings

Have you ever looked closely at the top of a tree stump? You might see many rings. The rings are often narrow near the center of the tree and wider near the outside.

Each rings stands for a year of growth. As a tree grows, more and more rings are added. After the tree has been cut down, you can see the rings on the stump. The number of rings tells the tree's age. The more rings there are, the older the tree is.

9 Which of these should you look at to find a tree's age?
- ○ The bark
- ○ The branches
- ○ The leaves
- ○ The stump

10 You would find few rings—
- ○ by looking at a tree stump.
- ○ in a young tree.
- ○ at the center of a tree stump.
- ○ in an old tree.

11 To tell the age of a tree, you must be able to—
- ○ sing.
- ○ write.
- ○ count.
- ○ read.

12 What is this story mainly about?
- ○ What tree rings mean
- ○ What a tree stump is
- ○ How to cut down a tree
- ○ Where to find narrow tree rings

The Cake Disaster

Valentine's Day is not my favorite holiday. People get so mushy. But my mom had made a really neat cake for our party. It had little silver hearts all over it. When you bit into them, they had chocolate inside.

Miss Andrews crooked her finger at me. "Andrea, your mother left a cake at the principal's office. Why don't you go get it?"

"My mother is bringing a cake, too. Can I go see if she left it?" The question came from Bernard.

Rudy smiled and I glared at him. Bernard always says his mother is bringing something for our parties. So far, she had not. But I guess Miss Andrews felt sorry for him, because she let him go with me.

When we got to the office, there was my mom's cake. I did fine until I tried to open the door and hold the cake too.

"Oh no!" cried Bernard. Splat! The cake landed on the floor, and some flew on the glass door. My face got hot. I was trying not to act like a baby and cry. That's when I saw a lady standing on the other side of the door. She had a big white box. Then I saw Bernard grinning from ear to ear.

13 At first, Andrea did **not** know—
- ○ that her class was having a party.
- ○ what kind of cake her mother had made.
- ○ where the principal's office was.
- ○ that Bernard's mother would bring a cake.

14 Who is telling this story?
- ○ Bernard
- ○ Andrea
- ○ Rudy
- ○ Miss Andrews

15 Why did Miss Andrews send Andrea to the office?
- ○ She thought Andrea was rude to Rudy.
- ○ She wanted Andrea to show Bernard the way.
- ○ She wanted Andrea to get the cake that Andrea's mother left.
- ○ She knew Andrea did not want to have a Valentine's Day party.

16 What happened to the cake that Andrea's mother brought?
- ○ Andrea dropped it.
- ○ Bernard fell on it.
- ○ The class ate it.
- ○ Bernard's mother took it.

17 What will most likely happen next in the story?
- ○ Andrea's mother will make another cake.
- ○ Rudy will laugh at Bernard.
- ○ The class will eat Bernard's cake at their party.
- ○ Miss Andrews will come to get Andrea and Bernard.

18 Which of these is another good name for this story?
- ○ "A Friend for Rudy"
- ○ "A Valentine Surprise"
- ○ "Bernard Learns a Lesson"
- ○ "Andrea and the Principal"

What did the old man find?

Long ago there was an old man. He lived by himself in a little house in the forest. Sometimes he was afraid to be alone. One day he found a unicorn at his door. The unicorn had a hurt leg. The man felt sorry for the animal. So he led the unicorn inside and took care of its leg. Then he gave the unicorn some warm milk. The unicorn thanked the man. It said, "I will stay and keep you safe." The man was never afraid again.

19 The man lived in—
- ○ a valley.
- ○ a city
- ○ a forest.
- ○ a cave

20 What did the man give the unicorn?
- ○ Some warm milk
- ○ A bowl of soup
- ○ A glass of water
- ○ Some fresh grass

21 From the story you can tell that the man was—
- ○ tall.
- ○ kind.
- ○ funny.
- ○ mean.

22 How can you tell that this story is make-believe?
- ○ A man could not live in a forest.
- ○ People do not talk to animals.
- ○ Unicorns are not real animals.
- ○ A man would not live by himself.

UNIT 4 Math Concepts

Lesson 8: Working with Numeration

Sample

    4   8   6   5
    ○   ○   ○   ○

STOP

1

2

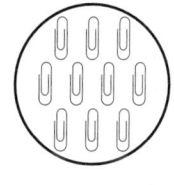 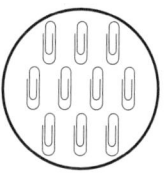 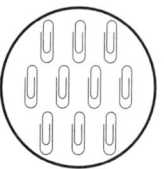 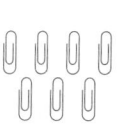

  37   73   47   38
  ○   ○   ○   ○

3

  11   24   21   15
  ○   ○   ○   ○

4

  69   40   35   53
  ○   ○   ○   ○

STOP

Primary 1

Lesson 9: Understanding Patterns and Relationships

Sample

| 3 | 6 | 9 | | 15 |

10 ○   20 ○   12 ○   14 ○

1

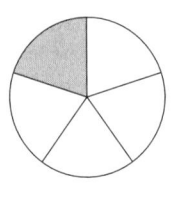

○   ○   ○   ○

2

| 35 | 40 | 45 | | 55 |

60 ○   54 ○   50 ○   46 ○

3

3 + 8 = 11   8 − 3 = 5   5 − 3 = 2   8 + 2 = 10
○   ○   ○   ○

4

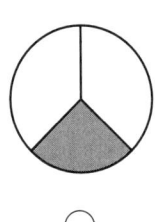

○   ○   ○   ○

Lesson 10: Working with Measurement

Sample

17¢   10¢   26¢   21¢
○   ○   ○   ○

1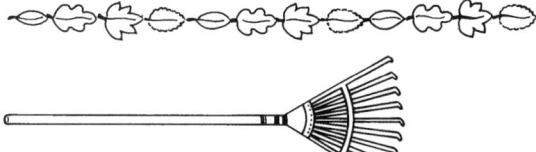

6   9   12   14
○   ○   ○   ○

2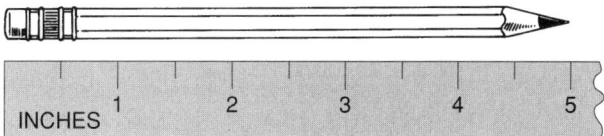

5   4   1   2
○   ○   ○   ○

3
	January					
Sun	Mon	Tues	Wed	Thur	Fri	Sat
			1	2	3	4
5	6	7	8	9	10	11
12	13	14	15	16	17	18
19	20	21	22	23	24	25
26	27	28	29	30	31	

1st   14th   7th   27th
○   ○   ○   ○

4

○   ○   ○   ○

Primary 1

5

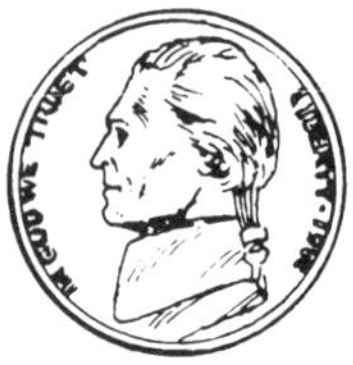

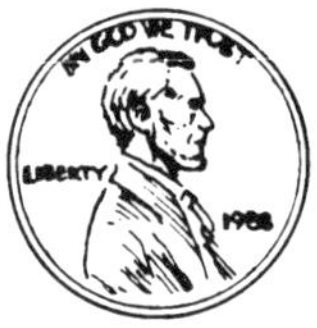

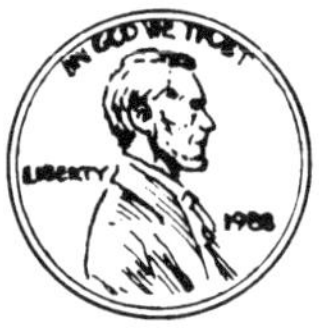

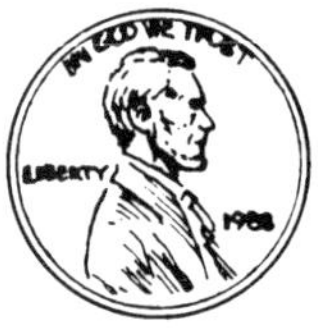

14¢ ○   8¢ ○   5¢ ○   10¢ ○

6

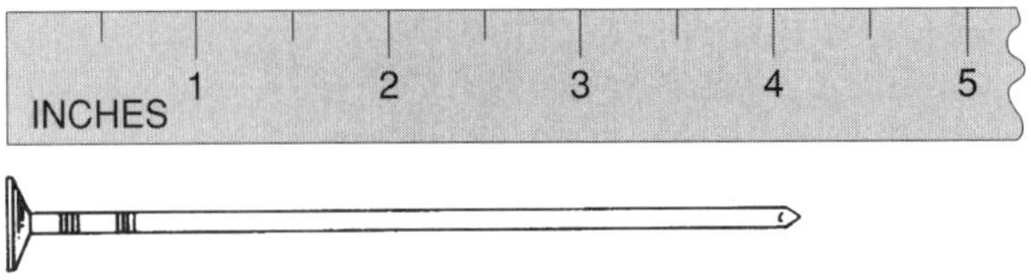

5 ○   3 ○   6 ○   4 ○

7

Sunday ○   Monday ○   Wednesday ○   Friday ○

8

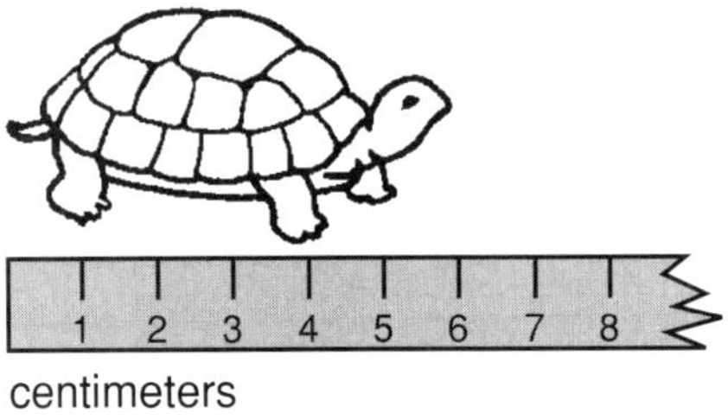

4 ○   6 ○   5 ○   3 ○

9

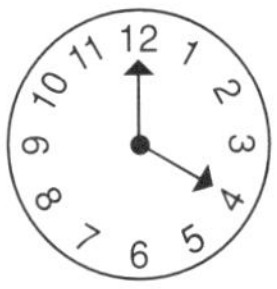

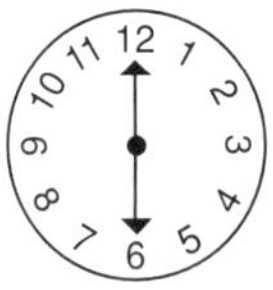

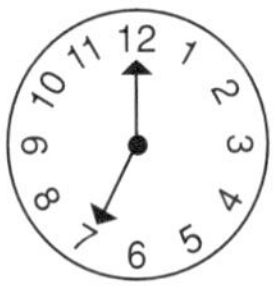

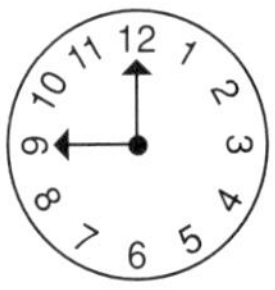

○   ○   ○   ○

Primary 1

Lesson 11: Working with Geometry

Sample

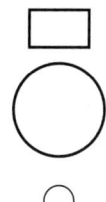 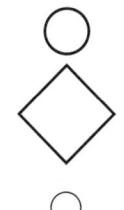  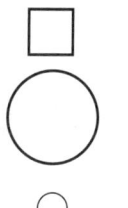
○ ○ ○ ○

1 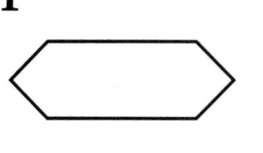   3   5   6   8
       ○   ○   ○   ○

2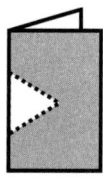
       ○   ○   ○   ○

3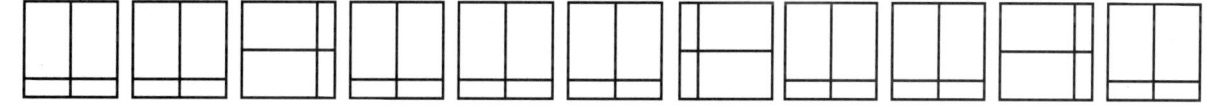
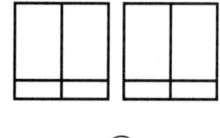   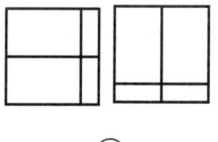   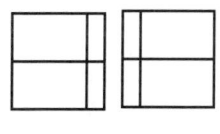   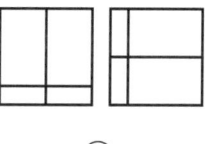
○   ○   ○   ○

4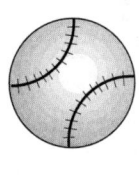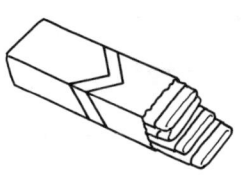
○   ○   ○   ○

Primary 1

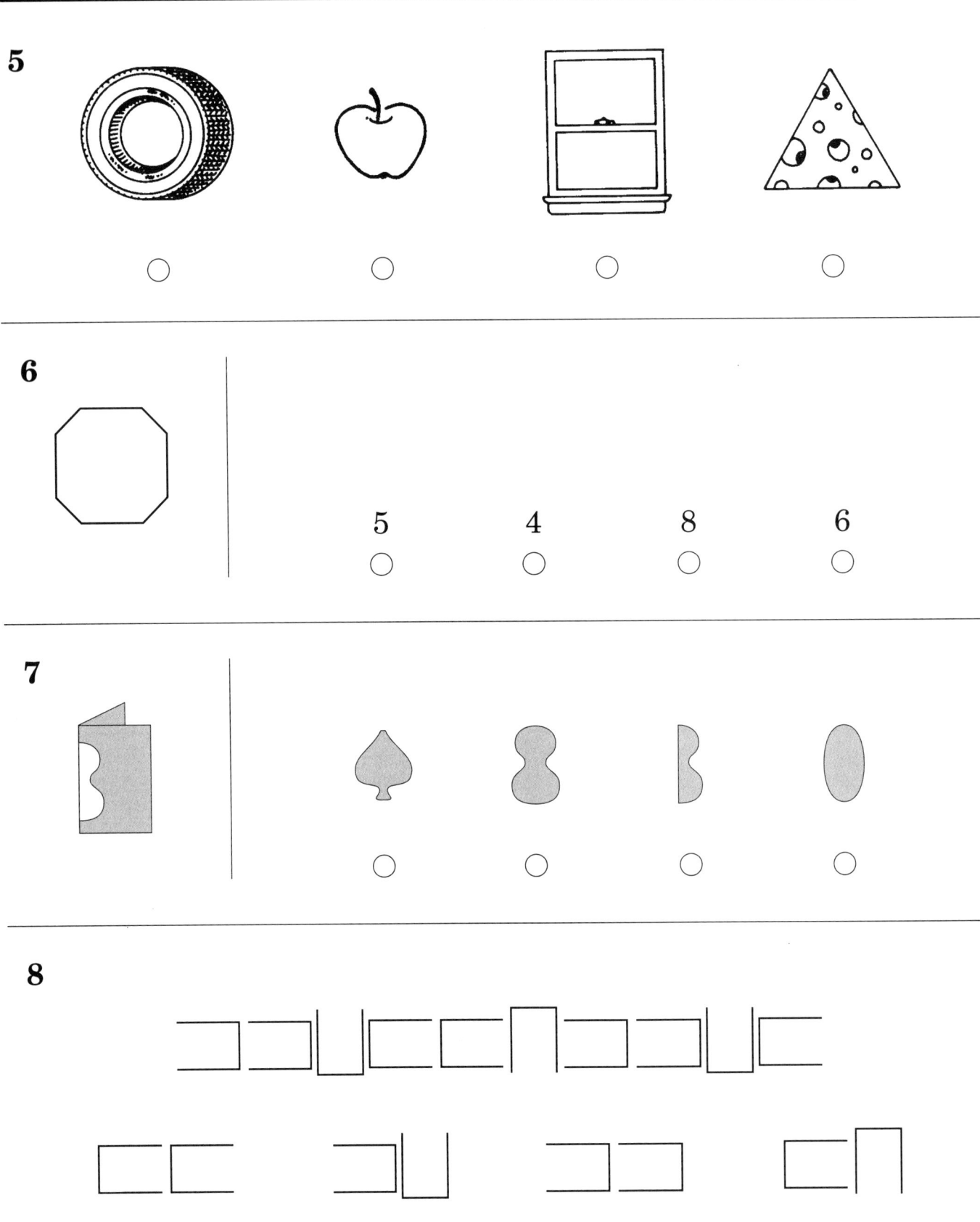

Unit 4 Test

Sample A

	7	9	8	6
	○	○	○	○

Sample B

25	52	502	250
○	○	○	○

1

third	tenth	ninth	eighth
○	○	○	○

2

604	46	64	640
○	○	○	○

3

14	23	24	32
○	○	○	○

Primary 1

4

| 38 | 41 | 52 | 33 |
| ○ | ○ | ○ | ○ |

5

| 26 | 31 | 29 | 15 |
| ○ | ○ | ○ | ○ |

6

| 75 | 50 | 62 | 44 |
| ○ | ○ | ○ | ○ |

7

| 85 | 71 | 67 | 94 |
| ○ | ○ | ○ | ○ |

8

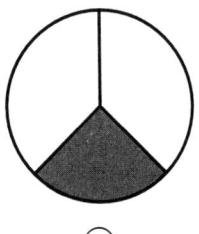 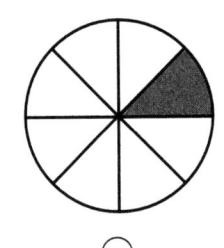 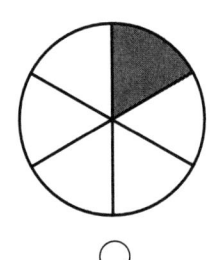

○   ○   ○   ○

Primary 1

9

65	69	73		81

76 ○   77 ○   78 ○   79 ○

10

39	42	45		51

46 ○   50 ○   48 ○   49 ○

11

6 − 2 = 4 ○   8 − 2 = 6 ○   6 + 8 = 14 ○   8 + 2 = 10 ○

12

3¢ ○   7¢ ○   12¢ ○   10¢ ○

13

17¢ ○   21¢ ○   13¢ ○   22¢ ○

14

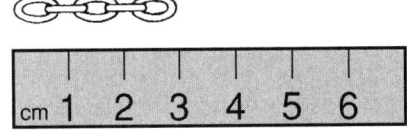

2	4	3	5
○	○	○	○

15

 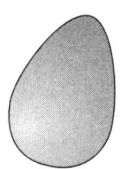  

○　　　○　　　○　　　○

16

3	5	2	4
○	○	○	○

17

○　　　○　　　○　　　○

Primary 1

34

18

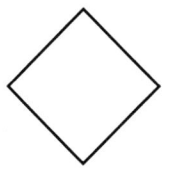

			16th		23rd		14th		21st
			○		○		○		○

19

20

○   ○   ○   ○

21

   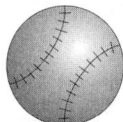      

○   ○   ○   ○

Primary 1

35

UNIT 5 Math Problems

Lesson 12: Working with Number Sentences

Sample

- ○ ☐ + 5 = 8
- ○ 8 + 5 = ☐
- ○ 8 − 5 = ☐
- ○ 13 − ☐ = 8

1

- ○ 9 − 4 = ☐
- ○ ☐ − 4 = 5
- ○ 5 + 4 = ☐
- ○ 5 − 4 = ☐

2

6 + 2 = 8   4 − 2 = 2   6 − 2 = 4   4 + 2 = 6
  ○   ○   ○   ○

Lesson 13: Solving Problems

Sample

1

    30   23   17   3
     ○   ○   ○   ○

2

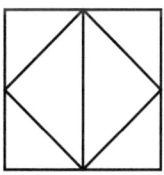   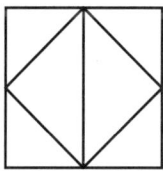   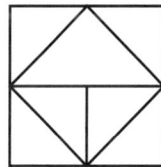   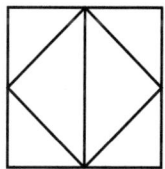

  ○   ○   ○   ○

3

   22¢   18¢   8¢   12¢
                         ○   ○   ○   ○

Primary 1

4

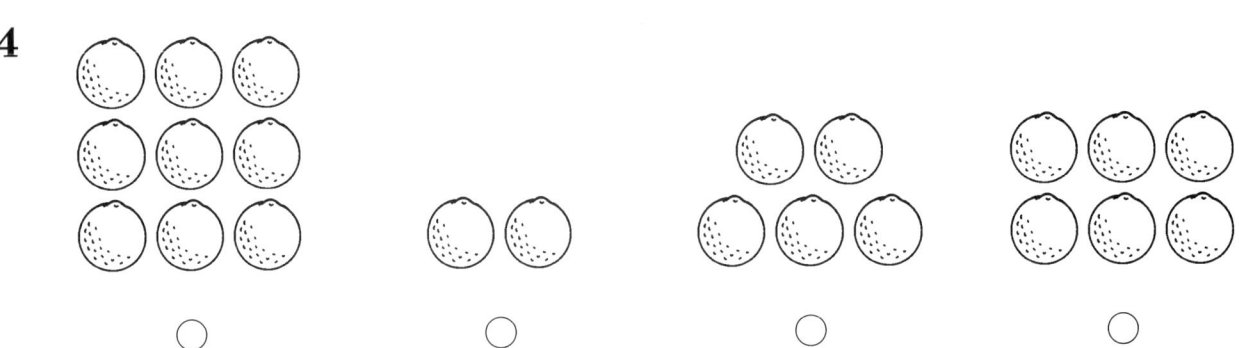

5

Lesson 14: Working with Statistics and Probability

Sample

○ ○ ○ ○

1

Each 🐻 = 2 bears

5   6   8   10
○   ○   ○   ○

2

Thursday   Friday   Saturday   Monday
○   ○   ○   ○

3

4   6   8   10
○   ○   ○   ○

Primary 1

4

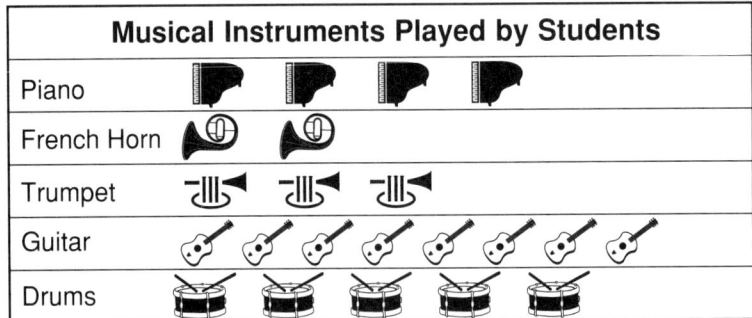

○   ○   ○   ○

5

| 4 | 9 | 7 | 8 |
| ○ | ○ | ○ | ○ |

6

| 3 | 13 | 11 | 5 |
| ○ | ○ | ○ | ○ |

7

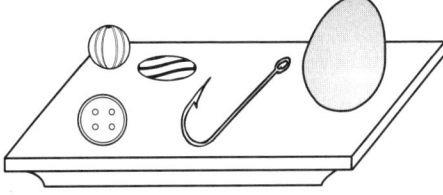

○   ○   ○   ○

STOP

Primary 1

Unit 5 Test

Sample

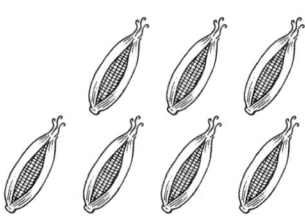

○   7 − 3 = ☐   ○   10 + 3 = ☐
○   ☐ + 3 = 7   ○   7 + 3 = ☐

1

○   13 − 4 = ☐   ○   ☐ − 10 = 4
○   10 + 4 = ☐   ○   10 − 4 = ☐

2

2 + 3 = 5   5 − 3 = 2   3 − 2 = 1   5 + 3 = 8
  ○   ○   ○   ○

3

      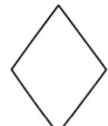   

  ○   ○   ○   ○

Primary 1

4

5

45	20	27	35
○	○	○	○

6

○ ○ ○ ○

7

9¢	11¢	4¢	19¢
○	○	○	○

8

  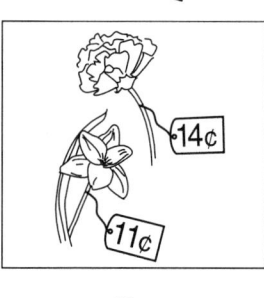

○   ○   ○   ○

9

Pet Store

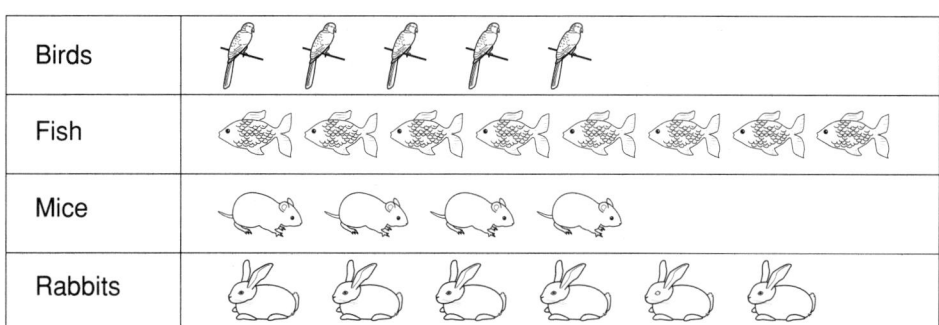

2	3	4	5
○	○	○	○

10

4   5   6   7
○   ○   ○   ○

11

1   2   3   4
○   ○   ○   ○

Primary 1

UNIT 6 Math Procedures

Lesson 15: Using Computation in Word Problems

Sample

| 8 | 6 | 3 | 2 |
| ○ | ○ | ○ | ○ |

STOP

1 9 2 🍊🍍 | 11   9   7   5
               ○   ○   ○   ○

2 15 7 📱 | 8   12   17   22
               ○   ○   ○   ○

3 14 15  | 1   11   29   36
               ○   ○   ○   ○

4 75¢ 50¢ | 25¢   55¢   60¢ $1.25
               ○   ○   ○   ○

5 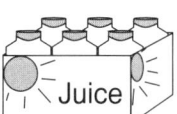 | 11   6   5   1
               ○   ○   ○   ○

STOP

Primary 1

Lesson 16: Using Computation

Sample

35 + 23   20 ○   40 ○   60 ○   80 ○

1

18 − 9 = ☐   5 ○   9 ○   11 ○   NG ○

2

10 − ☐ = 3   8 ○   6 ○   5 ○   NG ○

3

```
  7
  5
+ 3
```
17 ○   16 ○   15 ○   NG ○

4

```
  84
− 32
```
52 ○   46 ○   25 ○   NG ○

5

```
  42
+ 76
```
98 ○   118 ○   128 ○   NG ○

Primary 1

45

Unit 6 Test

Sample A

8 🐟	5 ○	10 ○	11 ○	13 ○
3 🐟				

STOP

Sample B

43	22	11	2	NG
− 31	○	○	○	○

STOP

1

9 🪲	13 ○	11 ○	5 ○	2 ○
4 🪲				

2

1 ○	5 ○	7 ○	9 ○

3

10 🦒	2 ○	4 ○	16 ○	19 ○
6 🦒				

4

16 ○	12 ○	7 ○	2 ○

GO ON

Primary 1

5 50¢
   30¢   2¢ ○   20¢ ○   60¢ ○   80¢ ○

6 49 − 23 = □   10 ○   30 ○   50 ○   70 ○

7 12 − □ = 3   8 ○   7 ○   6 ○   NG ○

8 8 + 5 = □   13 ○   9 ○   3 ○   NG ○

9
   8
   2
 + 6   14 ○   16 ○   18 ○   NG ○

10
   65
 − 51   41 ○   24 ○   14 ○   NG ○

11
   34
 + 95   129 ○   119 ○   109 ○   NG ○

UNIT 7 Language

Lesson 17: Building Listening Skills

Sample

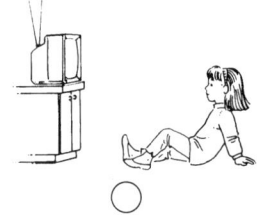  

1

2

3

 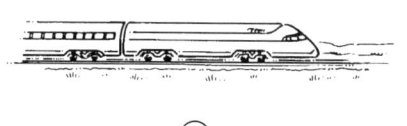 

4

Primary 1

Lesson 18: Prewriting, Composing, and Editing

Sample A

Julia's Ocean Trip

Julia's Journal
- Games we play on the ship
- Shopping in the market
- Swimming in the ocean

○   ○   ○

Sample B

We swam in the water.
And played in the waves.
We made sand castles.

○ We swam in the water.
○ And played in the waves.
○ We made sand castles.

Sample C

Shopping was fun.
Mother <u>buyed</u> me a hat.

bought   buy   Correct the way it is
   ○   ○   ○

Lenny's Horse

1.
   - ○ to tell why he loves horses
   - ○ to tell how to teach a horse tricks
   - ○ to tell a story about his pet

2. tricks ○   kiss ○   hand ○

Fun With My Horse

My horse can do many tricks.
He lifts his leg to my hand shake.
He gives me a kiss with his nose.
My horse can also play hiding games.

3.
   - ○ He lifts his leg to hand shake my.
   - ○ He lifts his leg to shake my hand.
   - ○ Correct the way it is

4.
   - ○ My horse is brown and white.
   - ○ I like to see my horse run.
   - ○ My horse comes when he sees me.

I <u>gived</u> my horse a treat after each trick.
　(1)

He <u>likes</u> carrots best.
　(2)

If I forget his treat, he shakes his head.

5　　gave　　　　　give　　　　　Correct the way it is
　　　　　○　　　　　　○　　　　　　　　○

6　　like　　　　　liked　　　　　Correct the way it is
　　　　　○　　　　　　○　　　　　　　　○

How People Travel

Table of Contents

1. On Tracks .....page 6
2. In Air............page 21
3. Over Land .....page 38
4. By Water.......page 50

7　　21　　　　38　　　　50
　　　　○　　　　○　　　　○

8　　1　　　　2　　　　3
　　　　○　　　　○　　　　○

Travel in the City

Many people drive cars.
In large cities.
Some people ride in taxis.
Most people ride the bus.

9
- ○ A few people might walk to work.
- ○ People work in a city.
- ○ The city is noisy.

10
- ○ Many people drive cars.
- ○ In large cities.
- ○ Some people ride in taxis.

<u>We lives</u> in the city.
(1)

<u>My father</u> rides a bus to work.
(2)

It is too far for him to walk.

---

11 We is living ○   We live ○   Correct the way it is ○

12 My Father ○   my father ○   Correct the way it is ○

Father's Birthday Surprise

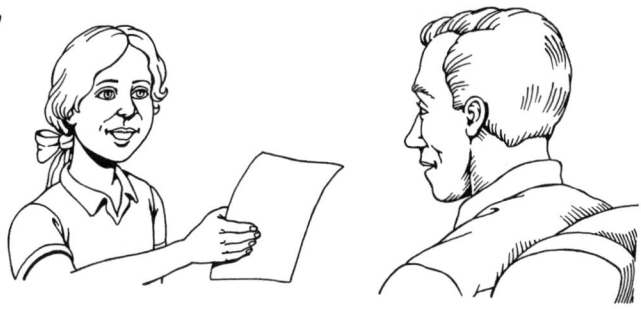

13 ○ bake her father a cake
    ○ make a list of things she does with her father
    ○ read a poem book

14 ○ a birthday party
    ○ a present Rita will give her father
    ○ things Rita likes to do with her father

Together

Together we have fun.
We laugh and we run.
We fish in the lake.
And Mother likes to bake.
Sometimes we go on hikes.

15 ○ And then we ride our bikes.
    ○ I am happy.
    ○ You are fun.

16 ○ Together we have fun.
    ○ We fish in the lake.
    ○ And Mother likes to bake.

Dear Father,
(1)
   Are you having a fun birthday
                          (2)
I wanted to make it special.
(3)
I love you.

Your daughter,
Rita

17 Dear father, ○   dear Father, ○   Correct the way it is ○

18 birthday? ○   birthday. ○   birthday! ○

19 I wants ○   I wanting ○   Correct the way it is ○

Lesson 19: Finding Misspelled Words

Sample
- ○ wint
- ○ along
- ○ ride

1.
   - ○ pickd
   - ○ these
   - ○ flowers

2.
   - ○ turn
   - ○ wash
   - ○ dishs

3.
   - ○ can
   - ○ cros
   - ○ street

4.
   - ○ Pleaze
   - ○ pass
   - ○ milk

5.
   - ○ frog
   - ○ gren
   - ○ grass

6.
   - ○ two
   - ○ babies
   - ○ playd

7.
   - ○ walkt
   - ○ store
   - ○ himself

8.
   - ○ boyes
   - ○ joined
   - ○ team

9.
   - ○ had
   - ○ party
   - ○ skool

10.
    - ○ wus
    - ○ eating
    - ○ apple

11.
    - ○ you
    - ○ see
    - ○ bakt

Primary 1

Unit 7 Test

Sample A

1

2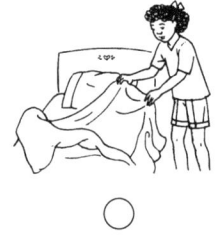

3

4

Sample B

A New Friend

Letter to a Pen Pal

- What Takashi looks like
- Why Takashi wants a pen pal
- Games Takashi likes to play

○ ○ ○

Sample C

Dear Paul,

I want to tell you about me.
I am in the first grade.
I like to play baseball.
Every day after school.

○ I am in the first grade.
○ I like to play baseball.
○ Every day after school.

Sample D

Will you <u>writing</u> soon?
I want to know more about you.
Your friend,
Takashi

write   writes   Correct the way it is
○   ○   ○

Primary 1

57

The Science Fair

5
- ○ buy seeds from a store
- ○ find a library book about seeds
- ○ go to a park

6
- ○ list ways seeds move
- ○ plant some seeds
- ○ glue seeds to paper

Animals Help Seeds Move
Some animals help seeds move.
Birds pick up seeds to eat.
They may <u>dropping</u> the seeds as they fly.
I have a new dog.
The seeds grow where they fall on the ground.

Primary 1

7
- ○ Some animals help seeds move.
- ○ Birds pick up seeds to eat.
- ○ I have a new dog.

8
- ○ drops
- ○ drop
- ○ Correct the way it is

> Some seeds stick to the fur of animals.
> They <u>dont</u> fall off easily.
> The ends of the seeds are turned up.

9
- ○ don't
- ○ do'nt
- ○ Correct the way it is

10
- ○ The seed ends look sharp and look like a fishhook.
- ○ The seed ends look sharp and like a fishhook.
- ○ The seed ends look like a sharp fishhook.

11   seeds   stick   sharp
          ○   ○   ○

The New Car

12 a red car   a safe car   wash the car

13
- talk to a car salesperson
- drive a car
- look under a car

A Safe Car

The car should be very safe. It needs seat belts in the front and the back. It must have new tires. The horn should honk. Very loudly for people to hear.

14
- ○ The car should be very safe.
- ○ It must have new tires.
- ○ Very loudly for people to hear.

15
- ○ The car will have two doors.
- ○ I want a car I saw at the store.
- ○ It should be a new car.

For Sale

I <u>have</u> a car for sale.
 (1)

It is in very good shape.

I need to sell it before <u>Thursday, june 28.</u>
                                                                                (2)

16   had ○   has ○   Correct the way it is ○

17
○ thursday, june 28
○ Thursday, June 28
○ Correct the way it is

18
○ Please call to find out more.
○ The car is sold.
○ I want to buy a red car.

Sample E
- ○ play
- ○ overe
- ○ four

19
- ○ livz
- ○ under
- ○ rock

20
- ○ pond
- ○ filld
- ○ fish

21
- ○ mean
- ○ what
- ○ sed

22
- ○ put
- ○ toyes
- ○ room

23
- ○ Mother
- ○ parkt
- ○ close

24
- ○ This
- ○ ende
- ○ line

25
- ○ told
- ○ funny
- ○ storie

26
- ○ fase
- ○ has
- ○ dirt

27
- ○ boys
- ○ splashd
- ○ water

28
- ○ bought
- ○ two
- ○ brushs

29
- ○ prety
- ○ pink
- ○ present

Primary 1

Comprehensive Tests
Test 1: Word Recognition

Sample A

car	also	chin	wait
○	○	○	○

1

daddy	neck	handle	dance
○	○	○	○

2

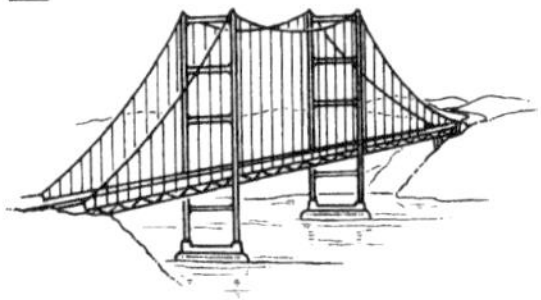

join	bride	ready	beyond
○	○	○	○

3

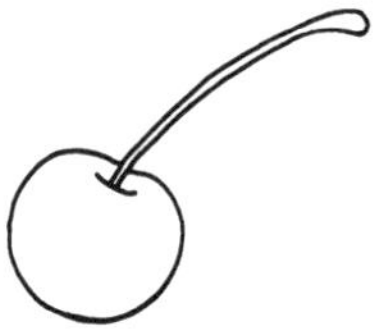

check	wonder	dollar	radio
○	○	○	○

4

mat	sweep	sled	wall
○	○	○	○

5

press	number	puddle	king
○	○	○	○

Primary 1

Sample B

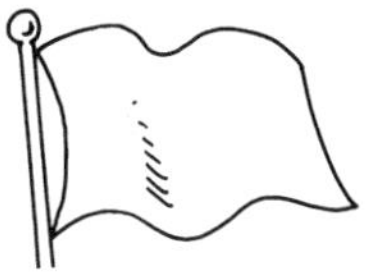

    cage   hug   garden   flower

6

    storm   forest   letter   smile

7

    key   really   fork   pony

8

    laugh   pillow   winter   tall

9

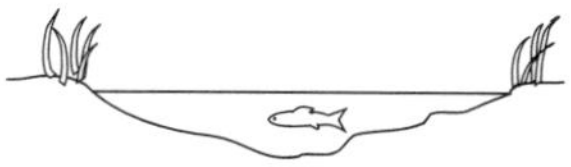

    grand   begin   listen   draw

10

    think   want   turtle   need

Primary 1

Sample C

f<u>i</u>ne
- ○ windy
- ○ side
- ○ rain
- ○ fit

STOP

11 b<u>a</u>king
- ○ crash
- ○ wave
- ○ dark
- ○ almost

12 j<u>e</u>lly
- ○ letter
- ○ please
- ○ seed
- ○ east

13 b<u>u</u>nny
- ○ tune
- ○ fruit
- ○ puppet
- ○ rule

14 r<u>e</u>ally
- ○ supper
- ○ best
- ○ season
- ○ desk

15 kn<u>o</u>ck
- ○ into
- ○ drop
- ○ cook
- ○ hope

16 n<u>i</u>ckel
- ○ bill
- ○ pie
- ○ line
- ○ write

17 d<u>ow</u>n
- ○ spoon
- ○ loud
- ○ won
- ○ port

18 bel<u>ow</u>
- ○ off
- ○ wore
- ○ form
- ○ sold

19 v<u>oi</u>ce
- ○ lost
- ○ song
- ○ toy
- ○ who

STOP

Primary 1

Test 2: Reading Vocabulary

Sample A
He wore a large hat.
- ○ tiny
- ○ big
- ○ funny
- ○ round

1 What time did she leave?
- ○ come
- ○ call
- ○ go
- ○ meet

2 Grandma lives in another city.
- ○ house
- ○ place
- ○ room
- ○ town

3 Please shut the window.
- ○ close
- ○ wash
- ○ open
- ○ fix

4 Jerry has a red auto.
- ○ coat
- ○ truck
- ○ car
- ○ bike

5 That fence is too high.
- ○ low
- ○ tall
- ○ strong
- ○ long

6 Go to the center of the room.
- ○ inside
- ○ edge
- ○ outside
- ○ middle

7 Rosa has many colorful fish.
- ○ tiny
- ○ several
- ○ two
- ○ big

Sample B

I like <u>this</u> park.

○ our
○ the
○ any
○ that

---

8 Mom was <u>glad</u> to see us.

○ careful
○ sad
○ surprised
○ happy

9 Which answer is <u>correct</u>?

○ wrong
○ yours
○ right
○ first

10 The bird flew <u>above</u> the roof.

○ below
○ over
○ around
○ onto

11 Libby was <u>first</u> in line.

○ not
○ always
○ last
○ never

12 Can you jump <u>over</u> this log?

○ above
○ under
○ behind
○ around

13 We want to eat <u>now</u>.

○ soon
○ then
○ lunch
○ something

14 Did you <u>send</u> a letter?

○ mail
○ write
○ open
○ receive

Primary 1

Test 3: Reading Comprehension

Sample A

- ○ Mother rocks the baby to sleep.
- ○ Father holds the baby.
- ○ Father reads to the baby.

1

- ○ The cat is napping.
- ○ A mouse jumps out of the box.
- ○ The cat is looking into the box.

2

- ○ Gabe feeds the ducks.
- ○ The ducks are flying.
- ○ Gabe plays tennis.

3

- ○ Carmen is eating lunch.
- ○ Carmen is jumping up and down.
- ○ Carmen has hurt her foot.

4

- ○ They watch the birds flying.
- ○ They are flying a kite.
- ○ Lee and Keiko play baseball.

Primary 1

Sample B
Working with Dad

Terri and her dad made little holes in the ground. They put a seed in each hole. Then they covered the seeds. Terri poured water on the ground. She said, "Now we will have good things to eat."

What were Terri and her dad doing?
- ○ Eating seeds
- ○ Watering flowers
- ○ Planting a garden

Marta's Special Day

Marta is having a party. Her father made a cake, and her mother blew up balloons. Marta's friends are coming and bringing gifts for Marta. Marta will blow out candles on the cake. Then everyone will have cake and milk.

1 What kind of party is Marta probably having?
- ○ A birthday party
- ○ A swimming party
- ○ A Halloween party

2 What is the story mainly about?
- ○ Marta's balloons
- ○ Getting presents
- ○ Marta's party

Sam and Kenji

My name is Sam. Kenji is my new little brother. After Kenji was born, Grandma came to visit from Japan. We live in San Francisco. Grandma stayed for three weeks. She met Kenji for the first time. I think she likes him better than she likes me.

Everyone in the family likes Kenji because he is so cute. They talk about him all day. I like him, too, but I want my family to like me again. I came first. I am five years old. I have a lot to talk about. Kenji cannot talk. He just sleeps in his crib or plays in his playpen all day.

3 Why did Grandma come to visit?
- ○ Her house burned down.
- ○ She wanted to see the new baby.
- ○ She wanted to travel.

4 Who is telling this story?
- ○ Sam
- ○ Grandma
- ○ Kenji

5 Where do Kenji and his family live?
- ○ Japan
- ○ New York
- ○ San Francisco

6 Everyone likes Kenji because he—
- ○ sleeps a lot.
- ○ is a sweet baby.
- ○ is the first child.

7 Which of these is another good name for this story?
- ○ "Kenji and His Playpen"
- ○ "A Visit from Japan"
- ○ "An Older Brother's Problem"

8 You can tell that Sam—
- ○ feels left out.
- ○ wants Kenji to talk.
- ○ wants to go to Japan.

How does the lighthouse help sailors?

Emily and her mother went to the beach in Cape May, New Jersey, last summer. One day they went to see the lighthouse.

Emily and her mom climbed to the top of the tower. From there they could see very far. They saw miles of ocean and beach. It was a beautiful sight.

Mr. Beal, the man who worked at the lighthouse, told Emily and her mom all about it. The Cape May Lighthouse is 131 years old. It is all white, and it is 165 feet tall. It has a very strong light. Mr. Beal said that the lighthouse is still very important to sailors. Sailors can see its light from 24 miles out at sea. The light helps ships come into Delaware Bay.

Mr. Beal told Emily and her mom how the sailors take care of the lighthouse. Their *tasks* are cleaning the light and making sure it is working. Mr. Beal said that many people who live in Cape May also help keep the lighthouse in good shape. They want others to enjoy it for many years to come. Some help fix parts of the lighthouse. Some clean the lighthouse. Others paint it.

Emily can't wait to visit the lighthouse again next summer. She wants Mr. Beal to show the lighthouse to her best friend, Jill.

9 Which words in this story tell what Emily and her mother saw from the top of the lighthouse?

- ○ …the man who worked at the lighthouse…
- ○ …people who live in Cape May…
- ○ …miles of ocean and beach…
- ○ …a very strong light…

10 What color is the lighthouse?

- ○ Blue
- ○ White
- ○ Yellow
- ○ Gray

11 Mr. Beal is—

- ○ a sailor who cleans the light.
- ○ the man who works at the lighthouse.
- ○ Emily's father.
- ○ one of the people who paints the lighthouse.

12 What does the word *tasks* in this story mean?

- ○ Jobs
- ○ Friends
- ○ Joys
- ○ Games

13 Why is it important to take care of the lighthouse?

- ○ So that Mr. Beal can have a job
- ○ To keep it safe for visitors
- ○ To help sailors at sea find land
- ○ So that sailors can see for miles from the tower

14 Which of these is another good name for this story?

- ○ "Emily and Her Mom Have Fun at the Beach"
- ○ "A Visit to a Lighthouse"
- ○ "Sailing in Delaware Bay"
- ○ "How to Take Care of a Lighthouse"

At the Circus

Patty went to the circus. She saw many things. There were three dancing bears. One of them wore a skirt. She also saw an elephant walk on its back legs.

Patty saw a tall clown in a little car. She laughed when the clown got stuck.

Patty looked up to watch people walking on wires. She sat very still. She was afraid they would fall.

Patty wants to visit the circus again.

15 What is this story mainly about?
- ○ Clowns
- ○ A trip to the circus
- ○ Elephants
- ○ Patty's dog

16 On how many legs did the elephant walk?
- ○ One
- ○ Two
- ○ Three
- ○ Four

17 Why did Patty laugh?
- ○ She thought the clown was funny.
- ○ She thought the bears were funny.
- ○ She thought the people on wires were funny.
- ○ She told a joke.

18 Where did people walk on wires?
- ○ On the ground
- ○ Over the water
- ○ In the air
- ○ On the back of the elephant

Mother's Day

Mother's Day was coming, and Maurice did not know what to do. He wanted to get a special present for his mother. But he didn't have any money. Then his sister said, "It's all right, Maurice. Not all great presents cost money." Then she told Maurice what to do.

Maurice walked through a field and along the road. He picked a beautiful bunch of wildflowers. He tied them with a red ribbon that his sister gave him. Then he gave them to his mother.

"Thank you, Maurice. They're beautiful," his mother said.

Maurice saw that his mother was smiling, and he smiled, too.

19 At first, Maurice does not know—
- ○ how to get a present for his mother.
- ○ how he was going to find his lost money.
- ○ that Mother's Day was coming.
- ○ how to pick wildflowers.

20 What lesson did Maurice learn?
- ○ He did not need money to get his mother a special present.
- ○ People should not waste money.
- ○ He and his sister should be nice to each other.
- ○ Walking near a road is not safe.

Test 4: Math Concepts

Sample A

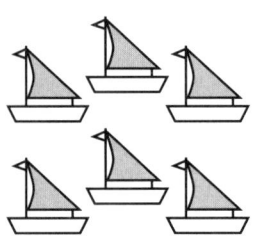

    4   6   8   7
    ○   ○   ○   ○

Sample B

| 43 | 46 | | 52 | 55 |

   47   50   49   51
   ○   ○   ○   ○

1

2

   18   10   13   16
   ○   ○   ○   ○

3

   56   65   75   66
   ○   ○   ○   ○

Primary 1

4

54	78	64	52
○	○	○	○

5

30	56	27	49
○	○	○	○

6

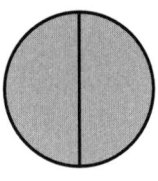 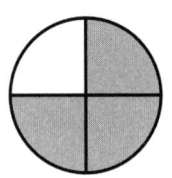 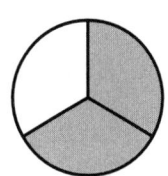 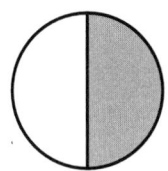

○   ○   ○   ○

7

65	70	75		85

76	84	80	90
○	○	○	○

8

$5 - 3 = 2$	$3 - 2 = 1$	$5 + 2 = 7$	$5 + 1 = 6$
○	○	○	○

Primary 1

GO ON

9

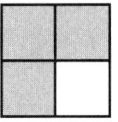 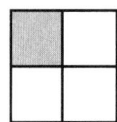 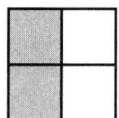 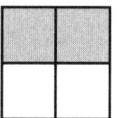

○ ○ ○ ○

10

○ ○ ○ ○

11

○ 11¢ ○ 21¢ ○ 7¢ ○ 25¢

12

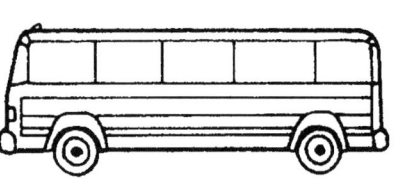

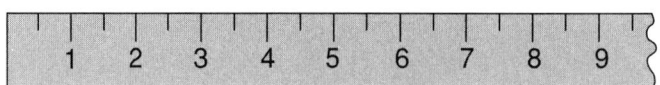
inches

7 5 6 8
○ ○ ○ ○

Primary 1

78

13

7	6	5	4
○	○	○	○

14

November

Sun	Mon	Tues	Wed	Thur	Fri	Sat
			1	2	3	4
5	6	7	8	9	10	11
12	13	14	15	16	17	18
19	20	21	22	23	24	25
26	27	28	29	30		

11th	22nd	10th	17th
○	○	○	○

15

○ ○ ○ ○

16

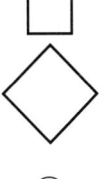 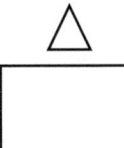 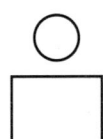 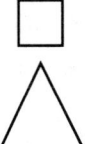

○ ○ ○ ○

Primary 1

17

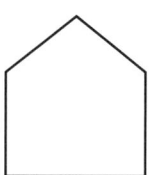

3	4	5	6
○	○	○	○

18

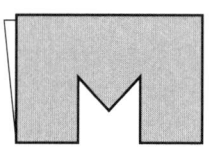

  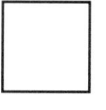  

○ ○ ○ ○

19

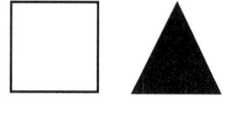

         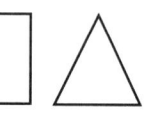

○ ○ ○ ○

20

   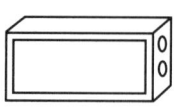

○ ○ ○ ○

Primary 1

Test 5: Math Problems

Sample

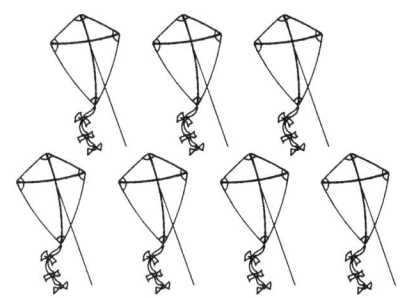 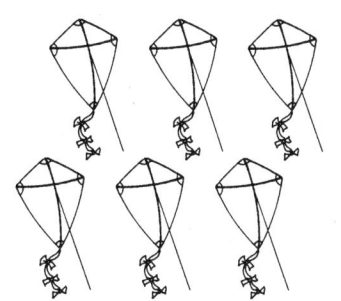

○ 7 − 6 = ☐   ○ 7 + 6 = ☐
○ 13 − 6 = ☐   ○ ☐ + 6 = 7

1

○ 8 − 2 = ☐   ○ 10 + 2 = ☐
○ ☐ + 2 = 8   ○ 8 + 2 = ☐

2

8 − 5 = 3   5 + 3 = 8   8 − 3 = 5   5 + 8 = 13
○   ○   ○   ○

3

○   ○   ○   ○

Primary 1

4

○

○

○

○

5

29　　　4　　　15　　　19
○　　　○　　　○　　　○

6

13¢　　8¢　　15¢　　11¢
○　　　○　　　○　　　○

7

○　　○　　○　　○

Primary 1

82

8

○   ○   ○   ○

9

Boxes of Seeds Jesse Sold	
Flower Seeds	🌸 🌸 🌸 🌸 🌸
Vegetable Seeds	🥕 🥕 🥕 🥕
Herb Seeds	🌿 🌿 🌿
Birdseed	🐦 🐦

Flower seeds   Vegetable seeds   Herb seeds   Birdseed
     ○   ○   ○   ○

10

    5   2   4   3
    ○   ○   ○   ○

11

    9   2   6   4
    ○   ○   ○   ○

12

    9   12   14   15
    ○   ○   ○   ○

STOP

Primary 1

83

Test 6: Math Procedures

Sample A

1	9	11	12
○	○	○	○

STOP

Sample B

$$\begin{array}{r} 68 \\ -13 \\ \hline \end{array}$$

45	51	81	NG
○	○	○	○

STOP

1

9
3

15	12	6	3
○	○	○	○

2

5
6

18	11	1	6
○	○	○	○

3

15
10

25	19	9	5
○	○	○	○

4

1	3	12	13
○	○	○	○

GO ON

Primary 1

5

   80¢
   60¢

| 2¢ | 20¢ | 60¢ | 80¢ |
| ○ | ○ | ○ | ○ |

6

42 + 37 = ☐

| 60 | 70 | 80 | 90 |
| ○ | ○ | ○ | ○ |

7

13 − ☐ = 9

| 4 | 5 | 6 | NG |
| ○ | ○ | ○ | ○ |

8

   9
   5
 + 4

| 14 | 15 | 16 | NG |
| ○ | ○ | ○ | ○ |

9

   78
 − 32

| 46 | 26 | 16 | NG |
| ○ | ○ | ○ | ○ |

Primary 1

Test 7: Language

Sample A

1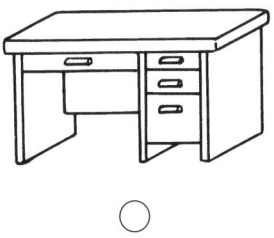

2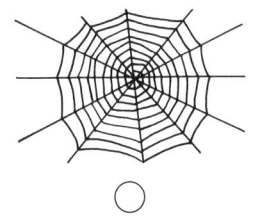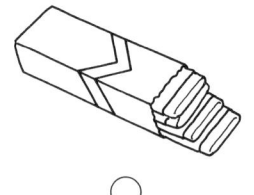

3

4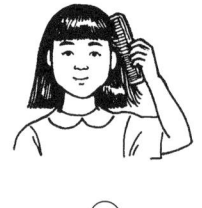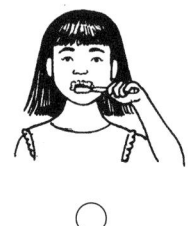

Sample B

A Favorite Holiday

The Fourth of July
- Go on a picnic
- Open presents
- Watch fireworks

○   ○   ○

Sample C

I like the Fourth of July best.
My family and I like to watch the parade.
After the parade, we go to the park.
To have a picnic.

○ I like the Fourth of July best.
○ After the parade, we go to the park.
○ To have a picnic.

Sample D

We <u>watches</u> the fireworks at <u>night</u>.
The colors light up the sky.

watch   watching   Correct the way it is
○   ○   ○

Primary 1

The Swimming Party

5
- ○ the time the party begins
- ○ the size of the pool
- ○ his house number and street name

6
when ○   wish ○   water ○

> Dear Sal,
> I am having a swimming party.
> It will be this <u>Friday, August 19.</u>
>   **(1)**
> Come to my house at 359 Pine Road.
> <u>We will much fun have.</u>
> **(2)**

7
○ friday, august 19   ○ friday, August 19   ○ Correct the way it is

8
- ○ We will have much fun.
- ○ We will have fun much.
- ○ Correct the way it is

Primary 1

You need to bring a swimsuit.
‎ (1)

I hope to see you.

Let me know if you arent coming.
‎ (2)

Your friend,

Mike

9   ○ needing   ○ needed   ○ Correct the way it is

10   ○ aren't   ○ are'nt   ○ Correct the way it is

Around Town

Table of Contents

1. What to See....page 3
2. What to Do.....page 10
3. Where to Eat..page 17
4. Special Activities.......page 26

11   ○ 10   ○ 17   ○ 26

12   ○ 1   ○ 2   ○ 3

In my town, you can visit a cave.
A train takes you under the ground.
A man tells you about the cave.
As you walk on a wide path.

13
- ○ A train takes you under the ground.
- ○ A man tells you about the cave.
- ○ As you walk on a wide path.

You can also go to the library.
Each <u>tuesday</u> they have a story time.
     (1)
<u>Someone reads</u> a story to the children.
(2)
Sometimes they have a puppet play.

14   Tues Day   Tuesday   Correct the way it is
      ○   ○   ○

15
- ○ Someone reading
- ○ Someone read
- ○ Correct the way it is

Primary 1

Summer Fun

16
- ○ to tell his friend how to sail
- ○ to tell what he did during the summer
- ○ to tell what he did at camp

Learning to Sail
I learned to sail a boat at camp.
We ate hot dogs.
First, you have to raise the sails.
The wind fills the sails.

17
- ○ The wind makes the boat move.
- ○ The camp is beside a lake.
- ○ The boat is big.

18
- ○ I learned to sail a boat at camp.
- ○ We ate hot dogs.
- ○ First, you have to raise the sails.

Sometimes the wind does not blow.
Guess what happens <u>then</u>
(1)
The boat will not move.
<u>Mr. sanchez</u>, the camp leader, must come get you.
(2)

19 then. ○ then? ○ then! ○

20 Mr. Sanchez ○ mr. sanchez ○ Correct the way it is ○

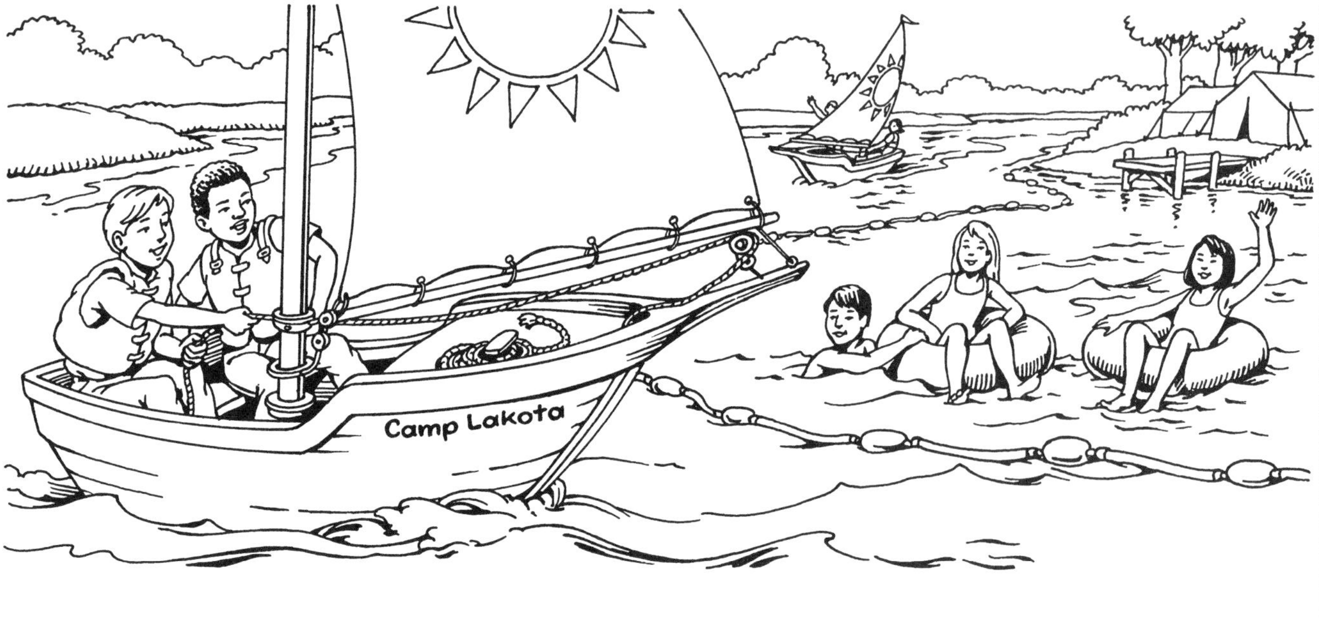

GO ON

Sample E

- ○ read
- ○ two
- ○ storys

STOP

21
- ○ packt
- ○ bags
- ○ trip

22
- ○ give
- ○ hir
- ○ turn

23
- ○ girl
- ○ three
- ○ wishs

24
- ○ children
- ○ playd
- ○ sun

25
- ○ win
- ○ first
- ○ prise

26
- ○ many
- ○ dayes
- ○ until

27
- ○ carful
- ○ wake
- ○ father

28
- ○ pick
- ○ toyes
- ○ leave

29
- ○ frend
- ○ riding
- ○ bike

30
- ○ fell
- ○ bumped
- ○ noze

31
- ○ teacher
- ○ calld
- ○ name

STOP